JAMES BROWN

Icons of Pop Music

Series Editors: Jill Halstead, The Grieg Academy, University of Bergen,
and Dave Laing, independent writer and broadcaster

Books in this series, designed for undergraduates and the general reader, offer a critical profile of a key figure or group in twentieth-century pop music. These short volumes focus on the work rather than on biography, and emphasize critical interpretation.

Published

The Velvet Underground
Richard Witts

Bob Dylan
Keith Negus

Elvis Costello
Dai Griffiths

Björk
Nicola Dibben

Buddy Holly
Dave Laing

Brian Wilson
Kirk Curnutt

Forthcoming

Elton John
Dave Laing

Joni Mitchell
Jill Halstead

Nina Simone
Richard Elliott

JAMES BROWN

JOHN SCANNELL

Published by Equinox Publishing Ltd

UK: Unit S3, Kelham House, 3 Lancaster Street, Sheffield S3 8AF

USA: ISD, 70 Enterprise Drive, Bristol, CT 06010

www.equinoxpub.com

© John Scannell 2012

All rights reserved. No part of this publication may be reproduced or transmitted in any form or by any means, electronic or mechanical, including photocopying, recording or any information storage or retrieval system, without prior permission in writing from the publishers.

ISBN: 978-1-908049-92-6 (hardcover)
ISBN: 978-1-84553-743-2 (paperback)

British Library Cataloguing-in-Publication Data
A catalogue record for this book is available from the British Library.

Library of Congress Cataloging-in-Publication Data

Scannell, John.
   James Brown / John Scannell.
      p. cm. - - (Icons of pop music)
   Includes bibliographical references and index.
   ISBN 978-1-908049-92-6—ISBN 978-1-84553-743-2 (pb)
1. Brown, James, 1933-2006. 2. Soul musicians--United States--Biography. I. Title.
   ML420.B818S32 2011
   782.421644092--dc23
   [B]
                                                   2011026490

Typeset by Atheus
Printed and bound in Great Britain by Lightning Source UK Ltd, Milton Keynes

Contents

	Acknowledgements	vii
1	A Musical Future	1
2	The Early Years	31
3	The Soul Era	53
4	The Foundations of Funk	77
5	The Godfather of Post-Soul	120
	Bibliography	151
	Discography	159
	Index	161

Acknowledgements

The book is always the product of many, and this one is no exception. Firstly, I would like to thank the Department of Media, Music, Communication and Cultural Studies at Macquarie University for its support of my project, and its assistance toward its research. For his particular help and guidance, I extend my sincere gratitude to the head of department, Mark Evans. Much of the initial research for the project was supervised by Andrew Murphie at the University of New South Wales, and his insight and dedication were vital to the consolidation of many of the ideas that appear in this book. My research provided the opportunity to make the acquaintance of James Brown archivists and scholars, Harry Weinger and Cliff White, both of whom were generous with their time and graciously answered all manner of questions, as did former Brown bandleader and architect of funk, Fred Wesley, of whom I was thrilled to be able to correspond and confirm content. There were, of course, many other interventions that would impact upon this book, and for their individual contributions, thanks must go to: David Bennett, Denis Crowdy, Chuck D., Peter Doyle, Jeremy Gilbert, Tony Mitchell, Charles Mudede, Charles Stivale and Lauren Wells. A special thanks must go to the series editors, Jill Halstead and Dave Laing, whose insight and experience have fortified the contents of the book. Further thanks must be extended to the production team at Equinox, including Valerie Hall, Sarah Norman and everyone else who helped to bring this project to fruition. Finally, I must thank my parents, Joan and John Scannell, for their eternal encouragement. I dedicate this work to them with all my love.

1 A Musical Future

On 25 December 2006 James Brown really *was* dead. Despite an earlier prognostication from LA Style, the Belgian techno group whose hardcore hit, 'James Brown is Dead' (1991), ensured years of wearying protestation to the contrary, this time the event had sadly come to pass. The tragic news loomed large over the holiday proceedings, as innumerable reports and tributes from global news agencies pervaded festivities. During these final days of 2006, those closest to Brown were busily scheduling his final tour; eulogies prepared, logistics in place, 'Living in America', presumably, now removed from the set list.

It was only fitting that the Apollo Theatre in Harlem, New York City was selected as the venue for the first public service. As the site of the famed album, *Live at the Apollo* (1963), and the venue synonymous with Brown's most renowned artistic achievement, Harlem's iconic theatre was a natural rendezvous for the many thousands of fans from around the country who had braved the frigid weather to join the seemingly endless queues to view the body. Hastily scheduled for 28 December 2006, merely three days after his demise, the embalmed corpse was delivered to the Apollo theatre in a glass-walled carriage and pulled by two white horses. As befitting a performer whose gruelling logistics were the hallmark of his career, the body was whisked off later that night, to Brown's hometown of Augusta, Georgia where it was awaited for two further ceremonies, public and private, to be held over the next two consecutive days.

Augusta's prominent public service, held at the city's own, James Brown Arena, was packed with compatriots past and present, an audience liberally scattered with popular music luminaries. Michael Jackson, for one, would emerge from a self-imposed exile in Bahrain, to make his first public appearance in the United States since 2005. His heartfelt eulogy echoed the sentiments of fans worldwide:

> James Brown is my greatest inspiration. Ever since I was a small child, no more than like six years old, my mother would wake me no matter what time it was . . . to watch

> the television to see the master work. And when I saw him move, I was mesmerized ... I have never seen a performer, perform like James Brown, and right then and there, I knew that that was exactly what I wanted to do for the rest of my life, because of James Brown (Jackson in BBC News).

Yet, despite the many plaudits of the visiting dignitaries, James Brown, as the people of Augusta were more than aware, was always the convoluted role model. His long-time residency in that city was one renowned for its scrapes with the law, and the performer's PCP-fuelled escapades of the 1980s and 1990s, threatened to eclipse a once esteemed musical, and political, legacy.

Introducing 'The One'

Brown's artistic impact persists to this day; for unleashing funk upon the world he will be forever recognized. The strange new implementation of rhythm originally to be heard on 'Papa's Got a Brand New Bag', and galvanizing 1967's 'Cold Sweat' and beyond, would mark the beginning of Brown's golden years of 1965–1975, as *the* most popular and cutting edge of any black artist. As Dom Foulsham was to remark in an article for *Blues and Soul* magazine, "[b]efore Brown, there was music with a beat. After Brown music had found a groove" (Foulsham 1993: 26). The drawing out of this "groove," leveraged, as it was, on "the one," would provide the key to much of Brown's subsequent musical success.

"The one" was a term used to identify Brown's signature emphasis on the *downbeat*, occurring on the first and third beats of a 4/4 bar, and responsible for shifting the rhythmic emphasis away from the second and fourth beats of the bar. Brown's emphasis on this characteristic beat would instil within popular music an unprecedented drive that would characterize not only the funk style, but also provide the rhythmic blueprint for dance music up to the present-day. Given the significant aesthetic ramifications of this musical gesture on the sound of contemporary popular music, Brown is hardly sanguine about his innovation, and has been keen to reassure the world of this: "I moved the music from two and four, to one and three with 'Papa's Got a Brand New Bag', which means all the music since '65, 95 percent of it, was copied from me" (Peterzell [dir.] 1995/Lawrence [dir.] 2005).

While never one to shy away from self-promotion, Brown's innovation cannot be so easily written off either. In the course of popular music scholarship, "the one" has endured its share of mythologizing; it is something of a musical enigma, its emergence seemingly without precedent. As Peter Guralnick recounts in *Sweet Soul Music*, Brown's origination of the funk style was derived from an almost mystical vision of purpose: "[h]ow Brown achieved this sense of security and mission remains as much a mystery today as it was in 1964 and 1965, when first *Out of Sight* and then *Papa's Got a Brand New Bag* sprang as full-blown new rhythm conceptions from their creator's mind" (Guralnick 1986: 221–22). Whether or not this "new bag" marks the actual invention of funk is moot. Indeed, the well-versed musical devotee might contend otherwise; that the real roots of funk can be heard in African-American musical styles pre-dating Brown, such as the "New Orleans beat" of Huey "Piano" Smith and the Clowns, and practised in turn by the drummer, Earl Palmer. The New Orleans style was, in fact, well known to Brown, arriving via his own drummer of the early 1960s, Clayton Fillyau. Prior to his tenure with the Godfather of Soul, Fillyau was previously acquainted with the Clowns and it is perhaps no coincidence that it was Fillyau who introduced the "New Orleans beat" to Brown's proto-funk cuts of the early 1960s, such as 'I've Got Money' (1962). Co-conspirator of the funk style proper, Pee Wee Ellis, could hear it too: "James did a tune early in the '60s called "I've Got Money." And *it's* funky. For him the thing was always there" (Ellis in C. Rose 1990: 47).

While the historical precedents to these formative funk gestures deserve due recognition, we cannot too easily discount Brown's seminal role in renegotiating a disparate palette of Southern musical styles, from gospel, to jazz and R&B into the powerful funk assemblage that it would become. A musical aesthetic that would come to serve as no less than the soundtrack of a burgeoning civil-rights era, and which would live on into the future as a source of inspiration to young African-American musicians, including, for example, the inventor of modern DJ techniques, Grandmaster Flash: "I was always very clear about something: no James Brown, no hip-hop, no me" (Grandmaster Flash and Ritz 2008: 241–42).

Through decades of DJing and digital sampling, Brown's jubilant rhythms have forged all manner of musical syntheses, contributing to the widely held belief that Brown is "the most sampled African-American recording artist in the history of recorded entertainment" (G. Brown 1996: 10). While the actual number of samples ceded to James Brown is perhaps impossible to accurately measure, at the turn of the 1990s, it was a number already estimated to be at least in the thousands (Weinger and White 1991: 44) and in the meantime is more likely to have approached the tens of thousands (Christensen 2003).

Such observations are indicative of how strongly Brown's musical pulse continues to resound through contemporary musical practice – a legacy so readily mandated that it moved DJ Shadow to write in the liner notes to his album *Endtroducing* (1996): "All Respect Due to James Brown and his countless disciples for inventing modern music." While a heartfelt and perhaps overly generalized tribute, Shadow's comments reflect a common assessment of Brown's musical legacy: "Whatever anyone says about Brown, however, he has exerted the greatest influence on modern dance music" (Brewster 1993: 66).

We have reached a point where many of Brown's refrains – the screams, the horn stabs, the "funky drummer" breakbeats – have been sampled so often as to have seemingly become part of the public domain. Lists of the many thousands of Brown samples used in electronic dance music genres are the subject of the rare groove cognoscenti, and inspiring of publications such as *Wax Poetics* and *Big Daddy* and dedicated websites such as *The Breaks* and *Who Sampled*. Despite an initial reluctance to embrace this new culture, the record companies were delivered a back catalogue bonanza, where obscure rarities would make up the legions of "breakbeat" compilations that have emerged in response to these new musical practices.

Brown's own record company, Polygram (now Universal), was quick to respond to the demands of the market. Its superlative *James Brown in the Jungle Groove* compilation, released in 1986, emerged as a direct consequence of the frenzied sampling of Brown that transpired in the mid-1980s. Buoyed by the record's success, this mining of the Brown back catalogue has been extended accordingly, resulting in further titles such as *James Brown's Greatest Breakbeats* (2005) and *James Brown's Funky People's Greatest Hits* (2005), as have transpired in the intervening years. Yet it was *Jungle Groove* that initially collected these tracks of underground arrogation, a selection that included the previously scarce funk motherload that was 'Funky Drummer' (1970) coupled with the 'Funky Drummer (Bonus Beat Remix)' which had the track's famous drum break, sequenced into a sample-friendly, two and a half minute mix.

Just as the main musical ingredients of hip-hop were slowly being turned over to the public at large, the blueprint for their digital resuscitation could be witnessed through the exemplary treatment afforded to them by hip-hop production teams, such as legendary Public Enemy producers, the Bomb

Squad. Discussing the almost ubiquitous appearance of Brown samples in the group's legendary 1988 album, *It Takes a Nation of Millions To Hold Us Back*, producer Hank Shocklee says Brown's 'Funky Drummer', "was my milk – like when you're baking" (Brackett 1997: 70).

In fact, electronic dance music producers' ongoing fascination and re-presentation of Brown's work has contributed to whole new genres of music. Referring to himself as an "overall product of the post james brown (sic) music generation," Ahmir "Questlove" Thompson, from hip-hop group *The Roots*, comments:

> it would be redundant for me to remind you of mr. Brown's (sic) anchor in classic hip hop ("funky drummer"), new jack swing (lyn collins' immortal "think (about it)"), drum and bass ("soul pride" accounts for at least 40 per cent of the genre's drum breaks) – or any of the offspring that these offspring offsprung (Thompson 2001: 16).

The exposure to Brown's refrains were exponentially related to the increasing affordability of digital sampling technology in the mid to late 1980s, which as Stetsasonic would argue on their track 'Talkin' All That Jazz' (1988), provided exposure to artists that might have been otherwise forgotten: "tell the truth, James Brown was old / 'til Eric and Rak came out with "I Got Soul" / Rap brings back old R&B and if we would not / people could have forgot." At the time of the song's release, Eric B and Rakim had had some major hit singles which had depended heavily on James Brown samples, in particular the Bobby Byrd sung, James Brown produced, 'I Know You Got Soul' (1971).

'I'm Real'

Increasingly piqued at hearing his voice emerge from the grooves of thousands of records that he had no relation to, nor gave any authorization for, Brown issued a musical retort. Hooking up with contemporary electro/R&B producers Full Force, he released the album *I'm Real* (1988), its confronting title track warning the samplers, "All you copycats out there . . . get offa my tip" and "take my voice off your record . . . until I'm paid in full". The latter a direct reference to Eric B and Rakim's, 'Paid in Full' that was a huge contemporary hit for the hip-hop duo, and lifted from an album borne of Brown's refrains.

6   James Brown

Designed to redress the unabashed replication of the sampling era, the *I'm Real* project sought to make this new generation of listeners aware of the actual source material for these apparently contemporary grooves. A victim of his own musical prescience, Brown's chastisements towards the samplers were wholly ineffectual, and begat more litigious strategies throughout the late eighties and early 1990s. As record companies began to initiate high-profile and well-documented lawsuits against emergent hip-hop stars such as De La Soul,[1] Biz Markie[2] and the Beastie Boys[3] the samplers simply delved deeper underground for increasingly obscure sample sources. Pinching from Brown was no longer worth the risk, and the unabashed sampling of his catalogue began to decline accordingly. Perhaps the samplers were put off by the stories that an entire floor of lawyers at Polygram were employed with the sole task of keeping track of the copyright infringements of Brown's catalogue. Even if the tale was apocryphal, it does serve to indicate the sheer level of illicit musical engagement that Brown's catalogue had been subjected to.

The legal pressure placed on the samplers may in fact have been a blessing in disguise, as by the early 1990s the use of James Brown samples had become widespread to the point of cliché. Into the fray arrives the aforementioned, chart-busting, techno hit, 'James Brown is Dead' (1991). Despite raising the ire of fans, the track was obviously somewhat of a backhanded compliment. To declare James Brown "dead" was to recognize a surfeit of Brown samples featured in the electronic dance music genres of the time,

---

1   De La Soul were sued over the song, 'Transmitting Live from Mars', from the album *3 Feet High and Rising*. Their track sampled a song titled, 'You Showed Me' by the 1960s band The Turtles. This is documented on the "Illegal Art" site: "The Turtles sued De La Soul in 1989 and won a judgement of $1.7 million. For its next album, De La Soul made sure to clear all samples, which cost a total of $100,000" (Farnsworth et al. 2002).

2   Also documented on the Illegal Art site/CD, "Gilbert O'Sullivan's 1991 lawsuit against Biz Markie for the uncleared use of 20 seconds from O'Sullivan's, *Alone Again (Naturally)*. The case proved a major turning point in the evolution of hip-hop. Markie lost the case; the judge told him, verbatim, 'Thou shalt not steal.' With that, the era of carefree sampling was over. Sample-heavy albums in the vein of Public Enemy's *It Takes a Nation of Millions to Hold Us Back* or the Beastie Boys' *Paul's Boutique* became impossibly expensive and difficult to release. Many artists continued to sample but retreated into using more and more obscure source material" (Farnsworth et al. 2002).

3   The Beastie Boys were also involved in one of the earliest sampling cases, as Adam Horowitz tells *Wired*: "You know, I'm pretty sure we were actually the first court case that used the word sampling in it. It was in a lawsuit involving a sample of Jimmy Castor's *The Return of Leroy (Part One)* on our first album" (Steuer 2004).

and to further comment on the rather unimaginative ways these samples were being utilized.

In *Living in America: The Soul Saga of James Brown* (1990), Cynthia Rose compared her subject to the seminal pop-artist, Andy Warhol, citing Brown as the "Andy Warhol of twentieth-century sound: a talent without whom it is simply impossible to try and imagine modern popular music" (Rose 1990: 16). While this connection is rather counter-intuitive, it is not as strange as one might think. If only because Warhol, the postmodern artist *par example* whose fame is similarly associated with industrial processes and copying, provides a necessary link to the productive mimesis that we will later encounter in this book as the "powers of the false," or the productive heterogeneity of musical styles that will transpire from the replication of Brown's refrains.

While the heyday of unrestrained Brown sampling might have waned since the late 1980s and early 1990s, this does not mean that it has, by any means, stopped. With a catalogue of 800+ songs, spanning a wide array of genres, Brown's refrains remain among the most persistent samples of a dance producer's arsenal. For this reason, tracks such as 'Funky Drummer' (1970), 'Think (About It)' (1972) and 'Funky President' (1974) remain ubiquitous elements of a diverse array of music styles. While the examples of their usage are simply too numerous to list in full, a brief survey might uncover tracks such as Pete Rock and CL Smooth's 'Da Two' on Pete Rock's *Soul Survivor* (1998), 'The Unseen' on Quasimoto's *The Unseen* (2000), and 'Natural Suction' on Wagon Christ's *Musipal* (2001) where the breakbeat from the 1972 Brown production, 'Think (About It)' is sped up to resemble a drum and bass track. This sample is a perennial favourite and can be heard on new releases every year without fail. In fact today's musical landscape is liberally peppered with Brown's refrains, whether this is to exhort a "get down!" throughout Trick Daddy's 'Take It to Da House' (2001) or having the 'Funky Drummer' beat cut up and reconstructed on tracks such as Daedelus's 'Lights Out' (2006) or K-OS's 'B-Boy Stance' (2004). While the more budget-conscious musicians have had to make use of Brown covertly, the high-profile artist with the money and the taste for old-school flavour will just pay the price for the sample. Tracks such as 'I Can' and 'Get Down', for example, from hip-hop performer, Nas's album *God's Son* (2002) both made prominent use of Brown's 'The Boss' (1973) while Chinese-American rapper, Jin, would use Brown's 'Blind Man Can See It' (1973) to establish his hip-hop pedigree in his debut release, 'Learn Chinese' (2004). Brown would maintain his currency with this new generation right up until his untimely death, and as well as the samples he was regularly called upon for guest spots on the albums of contemporary artists, such as that of the Black Eyed Peas' 'They Don't Want Music' (2005).

While it is easy to lambast sampling as a rip-off of Brown's material, as Stetsasonic argued on record, it did much to re-establish his public profile. The samplers' celebration of Brown's work not only drove the reissues of "rare groove" material, such as the *Jungle Groove* album but would, in turn, inspire a major remastering campaign in the 1990s. Prior to this renaissance of reissues, being a collector of Brown's back catalogue, even a few years earlier, was often a difficult endeavour. Outside of a few greatest hits compilations, the only other way to get hold of Brown's seminal albums was to pay though the nose for them at collectors' fairs and specialty record stores – a situation that has been significantly alleviated over the years thanks to the concerted efforts of Brown archivists such as Harry Weinger, Alan Leeds and Cliff White, who have been at the engine room of a superlative reissue campaign.

Sound of the Funky Drummer

Yet the reappraisal of Brown's work, and its introduction to the broader community, certainly owes a debt to sampling, which not only assisted in elevating Brown's profile, but also enabled some of his less well-known band members to get some of the recognition they deserved. As aficionados might contend, much of the work reincorporated as samples, are, despite their attribution, not just the work of Brown, but also that of the often unheralded musicians in his employ. For instance, the sampling success of the aforementioned 'Funky Drummer' was largely because of its drum break, the work of Brown's late-1960s sticks-man, Clyde Stubblefield. The 'Funky Drummer' drum break is so frequently sampled that is hard to concisely document how many times it has actually been used. In the liner notes for the superlative *Star Time* (1991) box set, it was estimated that even before the end of the 1980s, Brown's music had been sampled on two to three thousand tracks (White and Weinger 1991: 44) and it is safe to assume that Stubblefield's break was inordinately represented among this sample.

While the impromptu drum break was generating millions of dollars in revenue for the samplers, and for their record companies as well, everyone but the actual creator of the beat was benefiting from its appearance. Yet

Stubblefield had no share in the publishing, and he received no income from it, as the tune itself was solely credited to Brown: "When they used the James Brown 'Funky Drummer,' James owned everything at the time. No matter what I've done or what I played for that song. James got the money from the rap artists. But we didn't get it. But it's not money all the time, it's the respect" (Gladstone, Simins and Stubblefield 1997: 41). While Stubblefield would never receive any further remuneration for these appearances of his work, he has, at least, enjoyed worldwide recognition and consequently has been elevated to legendary musical status. Drawn out of comparative obscurity and thrust into the limelight, Stubblefield became the subject of many tribute articles. In 1990, *Rolling Stone* magazine awarded him "Drummer of the Year" because of the many instances of his work from decades past, including beats from 'Funky Drummer', 'Cold Sweat' (1967) and 'I Got the Feelin'' (1968), among others, which had suddenly reappeared as "new" releases in that year.

This new-found success would prompt further demand for Stubblefield's drum work by a new generation, allowing him to release his own sample CDs and midi drum beat packages, such as *DNA Beat Blocks: Clyde Stubblefield: The Funky Drummer* (1993), so that the contemporary musician could purchase a piece of his inimitable style. Those musicians with a budget could make use of the man himself, and Stubblefield would guest on Garbage's debut album, *Garbage* (1994), a group formed by fellow Wisconsonian, Butch Vig. Stubblefield's star has ascended to the point where he is no longer overshadowed by "the Boss," but receives his own musical tributes, provided through underground releases such as 'Good Old Clyde' by "nerdcore" hip-hop artist MC Sir Frontalot (Sir Frontalot 2005), or the *Sound of the Funky Drummer* by "Edan the Deejay" (Edan the Deejay 2004). As stated in the current (at time of writing) James Brown entry of Wikipedia, "James Brown remains the world's most sampled recording artist, and 'Funky Drummer' is itself the most sampled individual piece of music" (Wikipedia.com 2006).

It is well known that Brown was not the most scrupulous of employers, and the lack of musical attribution afforded to his former employees has always been a source of contention. Ex-members of the group have invariably suffered as their contributions were uncredited, or unpaid for, by Brown. Yet even those who have suffered this fate could still be positive about his artistic achievements. Take, for example, the ultimately gracious assessment of Brown by prominent ex-bandleader, Fred Wesley:

> Once you get away with something, you've set a precedent. And back there in the '60s, James set a hell of a precedent. All music that we hear today is influenced by James Brown. I stand on that – everybody today who calls himself a creator of music has been influenced by James (Wesley in Rose 1990: 37).

While the extent of Brown's legacy, musically, culturally and otherwise, continues to inspire, the simple fact is that, despite such enthusiastic proselytizing on Brown's behalf, there has been little sustained account, academic or otherwise, of the ongoing endurance of his musical innovations. To be sure, Brown has been the subject of several biographies, and his musical contributions have been referenced in numerous academic texts. Yet, of the titles available, none really brings these apparently disparate concerns into a sufficient and logical ecology.

The Literature on James Brown

The simple fact of the matter is that, when examining the scale of his musical impact, there is a relative dearth of investigative literature on Brown. In the article entitled, "Being James Brown" published in the June 2006 edition of *Rolling Stone* magazine (Lethem 2006), the author Jonathan Lethem writes:

> Someday, someone will write a great biography of James Brown. It will, by necessity, though, be more than a biography. It will be a history of a half-century of the contradictions and tragedies embodied in the fate of African-Americans in the New World; it will be a parable, even, of the contradictions of the individual in the capitalist society, portentous as that may sound. For James Brown is both a willing and conscious embodiment of his race, of its strivings toward self-respect in a racist world, and a consummate self-made man, an entrepreneur of the impossible (Lethem 2006).

While modesty precludes offering this tome as the reflection of such an exacting brief, this book does try to make amends for the apparent shortfall in the available literature, which constitutes one of popular music's most egregious blindspots. For many years there was really only a single book on Brown available, his own autobiography, *The Godfather of Soul* (1986) as told to Bruce Tucker (and timed to coincide with Brown's induction into the rock'n'roll hall of fame). While Brown would, rather strangely, do it all again in another account titled, *I Feel Good* (2005), the results would net negative returns the second time around. The latter title, almost certainly ghost written by co-author, Marc Eliot, is full of factual errors and inconsistencies. Music writer and James Brown aficionado, Douglas Wolk, who in 2004 would write his own book on Brown's *Live at the Apollo* album, writes in his review of the book, "If, for some reason, Eliot was unclear about this stuff, he could have checked it by looking at the older book – or the liner notes of any number of James Brown CDs" (Wolk 2005). Suffice to say, the book is best avoided.

While the biography has its place, by their very nature, biographical accounts are limited in regard to a more rigorous accounting of the ontological considerations of their subject's work; that is to say, the process of how things *become* rather than simply recounting a series of historical events.

Articulating decisive links between Brown's work and the DJ culture that embraced it so emphatically might be the first way to make amends for the shortfall. For even during the watershed years for the sampling of James Brown's music, a period spanning the late 1980s to early 1990s, there was still a relative drought in terms of theoretical documentation. In fact the only book to appear at that time is the excellent, and now sadly out-of-print, *Living in America: The Soul Saga of James Brown* (1990) by Cynthia Rose. Rose's account was the first attempt to illustrate Brown's ongoing effect on contemporary music and the then burgeoning sampling culture. In addition, the book also provided some of the first insider accounts of working with Brown to be had at the time. Rose draws on interviews with Brown and his former band members, in an attempt to unearth the roots of what she refers to as Brown's "surrealistic" musical outlook (Rose 1990: 38–39). Rose's enticing proposition is unfortunately never extrapolated explicitly, which is somewhat of a pity, as Brown's music provides testament to the pursuit of the unorthodox. An extrapolated defence of this very idea is contained in Chapter 5 of this book. Suffice to say, this oversight does not detract from my enthusiasm for Rose's book which is perhaps the most engaging, critically informed profile of Brown yet available.

Inspired perhaps by the wave of sampling of Brown's music in the preceding decade, the 1990s served Brown fans somewhat better, as more titles did begin to appear, and in relatively close proximity. One noteworthy entry was

Geoff Brown's *James Brown: Doin' It to Death* (1996), which provided the most encompassing biographical profile yet, based as it was on decades of research undertaken by world-renowned Brown scholar (and confidante), Cliff White. In the same year, another, equally illuminating, text appeared, Rickey Vincent's award-winning *Funk* (1996). However, this title was more concerned with a broader overview of the funk genre in general, condensing Brown's contribution to the genesis of the style into the space of a chapter. It should be noted, however, that prior to Vincent's publication, the funk genre had been subject to relative theoretical neglect, and, as Vincent himself pointed out, his book attempted the first dedicated text on the genre (Vincent 1996: xvii). As such, *Funk* attempted to trace the evolution of Brown's "One" into an aesthetic, through an erudite genealogical account that previously had to be gleaned from a myriad of disparate sources.

Brown's invention tended to become subsumed by more general accounts of the soul aesthetic, although even these texts were few and far between. Of these titles, an early and perhaps more esoteric title was Michael Haralambos's *Right On: From Blues to Soul in Black America* (1974). Haralambos discusses the emergence of soul and its impact and decline through chart statistics. While Haralambos's work is overtly empirical in nature, Gerri Hirshey's *Nowhere to Run* (1983) on the other hand, would proffer a series of contemporary portraits of the major artists to emerge in the soul period. At the time of writing, in the early 1980s, many of Hirshey's subjects, left in the dust of Disco hysteria, were considered as "washed up" as the soul aesthetic they once espoused. Hirshey's detailed portraits capture much of the pathos of life after the soul years. Written in the early 1980s, the book captures an interesting transitional period, appearing as it does just prior to the sampling culture that would re-energize the public profiles of many of her subjects.

Following Hirshey's book was another equally noteworthy entry in the field, Peter Guralnick's *Sweet Soul Music* (1986). Guralnick's book provided a comprehensive historical account of the rise of the soul music style. Just as one would expect, *Soul Brother No. 1* (Weinger and White 1991: 41) is inordinately represented throughout Guralnick's account, although given the scale of the soul project, the Brown story is mostly confined to a lengthy chapter.

To get closer to understanding what might have driven Brown's musical experimentation, one might turn to former Brown bandleader Fred Wesley, whose *Hit Me, Fred: Recollections of a Side Man* (2002) has provided an illuminating addition to the still comparatively slim body of Brown scholarship.

Wesley's book provided the first detailed descriptions of what it was like to operate as part of the James Brown machine. Wesley's book does not disappoint, providing an insider account of the arduous, and mostly unnecessary, around-the-clock band rehearsals demanded by Brown, and rather more surprisingly, an expression of the contempt that Brown's band members felt for their leader and his music.

Unsurprisingly perhaps, Brown has been better served after his death than before it. In recent years there has been several new books released including the handy compendium, *The James Brown Reader: Fifty Years of Writing about the Godfather of Soul* (2008) containing a series of articles on Brown spanning the length of his career, edited by prominent music writer Nelson George, and former Brown alumni, Alan Leeds. Also released was *The Hardest Working Man: How James Brown Saved the Soul of America* (2009), a book that accompanies the anniversary of Brown's city-saving 1968 Boston Garden performance (more of this later), as well as *Say It Loud! My Memories of James Brown Soul Brother No.1* (2009) by Augusta Chronicle journalist and long-time associate, Don Rhodes. While the latter looks like a cheap cash-in, it is actually a deceptively detailed history of Brown's biography and life in and around his hometown of Augusta, Georgia.

However, with the exception of Cynthia Rose's book, which makes the odd reference to postmodernism and critical theory, there was no sustained academic account of Brown's work, that is, until the appearance of Anne Danielsen's *Presence and Pleasure: The Funk Grooves of James Brown and Parliament* (2006). Danielsen dedicates much effort to the assimilation of the often disparate disciplinary goals of musicology and philosophy and the book provides a broad but accessible overview of those Western aesthetic values that have conspired against a more comprehensive appreciation of black music. Danielsen's commentary shares a similar interdisciplinarity to my own research on Brown, and makes use of Deleuzean concepts of difference and repetition and its relation to the constitution of the experience of the groove. While the chapters on non-linearity and its effect on experience of temporality presents some of Danielsen's most inspired theoretical exegesis, one of the main problems of the book was the author's willingness to embrace some of the essentialist proselytizing that has emerged from certain sections of African-American music scholarship. For example, Danielsen's embrace of Nelson George's arguments on funk's apparent emasculation at the hands of the "crossover" impulse in the mid-to-late 1970s as evidence of the "dilution" of funk's "blackness" (Danielsen 2006: 97). That Danielsen chooses to accept this type of essentialism at face value merely subsumes her own compelling evidence of black music's stylistic bifurcations and cultural *becomings* that emerge throughout her study. Such ethnocentrically focused discussions of funk invariably promote an unnecessary fixation on essentialized racial identity, which unnecessarily detracts from the imminent (and immanent) circumstances that produced the music.

A particularly egregious example of essentialism can be found in David Brackett's "James Brown's *Superbad* and the Double-voiced Utterance" (1992). In this analysis, Brackett offers up James Brown's *Superbad* (1970), as somehow significant of the "critical difference" that exists between African-American and Euro-American compositional approaches (Brackett 1995: 156). In short, Brackett has Brown stumbling upon an apparently improvised compositional approach that rather miraculously adheres to the mathematical proportions of the so-called Golden Section (of which Brackett asserts that James Brown's "Superbad" conforms to aesthetically by maintaining a ratio of 0.618 to 1) (Brackett 1995: 152). This will lead to Brackett's observation that Brown's "naturalness" allows him to achieve the same results as the "calculated" composition of European art musics (Brackett 1995: 154).

Noted musicologist Philip Tagg singles out Brackett's essay for criticism; in particular, what he sees as the "essentialisation of ethnic characteristics in music" (Tagg 1998) taking particular offence at Brackett's ascription of a generally unspecified "Africanness" in Brown's music, declaring that: "Brackett knows there is a problem but seems sometimes to be trapped within it. The terms of reference defining this problem need to be criticized and widened to make real historical sense" (Tagg 1998).

This type of ethnic essentialism has been inherent to the genealogical approaches to Brown's music that simply reify its aesthetic constitution into more general "African" characteristics, for example, Craig Werner's study of soul music, *A Change is Gonna Come*, which features passages such as: "there's no doubt that once the Godfather of Soul took his rhythm stick to 'the one', American music became something different, blacker, and more African than it had ever been before" (Werner 2000: 25). This is reiterating a simple and essential commentary that had been doing the rounds for some years, just as Miles Davis remarks here: "the Real Thing was James Brown . . . Brown was proof that black people were different. Rhythmically and tonally blacks had to be from somewhere else. Proof that Africa was really over there for those of us who had never seen it – it was in that voice . . ." (Davis in Guralnick 1986: 243).

There are more productive ways of accounting for Brown's invention than attributing it a spurious ethnic identity. That is not to say that funk does not constitute an important artistic gesture emanating from the African *diaspora*, but the conditions for its invention need a specificity beyond a simple "African" reification. For Brown himself would profess to have little idea as to why his music was being compared with African musical forms: "I went over there and I heard their thing, and I felt their thing. But I honestly hadn't heard their thing in mine" (Rose 1990: 126). While funk's relationship to his past will be dealt with in detail later in the book, for present purposes it is posited that Brown's retort is not simply one of denial, but instead signals the complexity of identity which implores further discussion. A complexity that has been limited through the more essentialist discourse that his work has suffered from. This essentialism might, for example, take the form of the disturbing inclination to perpetuate a false dichotomy that attributes an "authenticity" to funk that is judged against the "artificiality" of electronic music practices, evident in the following excerpt from Rickey Vincent's book *Funk* (1996):

> Funk returned to the ideals of the African ensemble just as technology began to push American music toward artificiality. Just as the electric Fender Rhodes piano, the Moog synthesizer, Hohner clavinet, and ARP ensemble synthesiser were introduced into black popular music, the conga player, percussion section, Kalimba, and the extended jam were also incorporated. Funk became the medium by which electronic sound effects never before heard on synthesisers of the future could be channelled through a black aesthetic, complemented by traditional sounds of the past, creating a better understanding of the present. From the extremes of a simple drumbeat, to orchestrated polyphonic arrangements played by multiple musicians in unison, to a celebration of deep individual expression, funk music was arranged to bring "soul" to the people through the new formulas of popular music (Vincent 1996: 19–20).

While Vincent's book deserves credit for at least attempting an analysis of *Funk*, its overall gesture of attributing the form with the status of quasi-religious Afrocentric experience might be poetically sound, but, conceptually, it is somewhat lacking. Further to this, Vincent's preoccupation with dichotomizing funk from the electronic disco aesthetic (of which his beloved Parliament-Funkadelic was absolutely a major influence) means that funk's ontology is unnecessarily discriminatory. A more reasonable argument might contend that it was precisely black music forms, and funk in particular, that introduced many of the compositional elements that were subsequently capitalized upon by electronic music. For rather than dichotomizing funk and the electronic, the most pertinent gesture would be to bring them closer together. For Brown's funk impelled an unprecedented, almost clockwork, exactitude and precision to popular music, which, as former Velvet Underground member, John Cale, argues, is almost extra-human in its capacity:

> ... it was a search for perfection... He would say, "If you play the wrong note I'm going to dock your pay one hundred dollars!" There was a kind of mentality of absolute exactitude. The electric metronome came in and it would not change by one iota. It was rigid all the way through (Cale in Gilbert and Pearson 1999: 123).

In his article, "Sample and Hold: Pop Music in the Age of Digital Reproduction," Andrew Goodwin will proclaim that, "[w]e have grown used to connecting machines and *funkiness*" (Goodwin 1990: 263), yet it is extremely curious that Goodwin makes no attempt to show how African-American artists, and perhaps Brown especially, would help to create that very connection between funk and the machine. This is a source of contention for Tricia Rose, who criticizes Goodwin's oversight in her book, *Black Noise* (1994):

> [Goodwin] refers to four major contemporary black dance forms – disco, hip hop, Hi-NRG, and house – as the bases for his argument regarding the way in which technology is made funky and the community-based nature of these forms without one reference to black cultural priorities, black musical traditions, or black people. He makes no mention of black practitioners and the possibility that these dance artists are using sampling technology to articulate black approaches to sound, rhythm, timbre, motion, and community (Rose 1994: 84).

A Musical Future 17

This symbiosis of funkiness and technological expression, and the vital role Brown plays in its connection, are central to the discussion of this book, which further extrapolates this idea that musical technologies are a direct consequence of affordances such as "black approaches to sound, rhythm, timbre, motion, and community" that Rose refers to, and which subsequently beckon the appropriate machines to take them up.

Of course when it came to machinic, super-human precision, one need look no further than the James Brown bands, whose inordinate contribution is affirmed here by Led Zeppelin's John Paul Jones:

> The precursor to all modern dance music. James tried to get his band to play like a machine. The rhythm section just kicked over all the time. When machines did came intro dance, music people complained that the sound wasn't real or soulful, but here was James Brown pushing his band into playing as tightly as a machine. He was a tyrant as a bandleader- he forced his band to play exactly what he wanted where he wanted it . . . It was a groove machine! I liked his other tunes like *Papa's Got a Brand New Bag* but this was the future. Kids today understand how to put a groove together like they didn't in my day and it's all down to James Brown (Harrington and Jones 2002: 16).

In light of Jones's assessment, it is fair to say that the almost superhuman intricacy and precision of Brown's bands of the time foreshadow no less than a new musical paradigm, and, moreover, one that indicated something of dance music's technological future.

Commonplace as it is to bestow upon groups, such as Kraftwerk, electronic dance music's aesthetic legacy, Brown's role in the creation of the very rhythmic affordances that would be taken up by these electronic instruments certainly deserves a more detailed commentary. The sheer exactitude of Brown's grooves prophesied new methods of technological replication, as few mortals could manage the meticulous rhythms that underpinned his style. As former Kraftwerk drummer, Wolfgang Flür, would comment in the documentary *Better Living Through Circuitry* (1999), the group's invention of an electronic kit was to make life easier: ". . . very elegant you know, without sweating" (Flür in Reiss [dir.] 2001).

While the aesthetic ramifications of the Protestant Work Ethic might have assisted with popular music's technological makeover, the precedent of rhythmic exactitude was already long in place. And for that, James Brown is owed much thanks. Accordingly, this book attempts to more readily integrate the still underdeveloped discussion of Brown's pivotal role in instigating such machinic intervention, as his funk would set vital precedents for the new structural logic of popular music from the 1970s and onward.

Brown's subjection to dichotomizing, as illustrated by Vincent's opposition of soul to the "artificiality" of machines, has only served to "other" Brown from the enormous impact he has had on producing a future for electronic music composition. While not necessarily a pioneer in utilizing electronic instruments in the way that one might think of Stockhausen or Schaeffer, Brown's approach to rhythm was an essential ingredient to the aesthetics of electronica. Brown's commitment to experimentation was precisely the attribute that would set him apart from the soul performers that emerged from similar aesthetic circumstances, Ray Charles, Wilson Pickett or Al Green for example. For it is in the galvanization of the form that Brown can legitimately claim to have harnessed the power of the funk into a force of *becoming*, and one that would connect to the future with much greater force than the contributions of his closely related musical peers and contemporaries. This is why this book attempts to show how Brown's work might be better considered through an evaluation of what his music would give to the future, rather than what it took from the past. Such a proposal should not be understood as a discounting of Brown's musical or cultural inheritance, but rather as a reflection of his own commitment to insist upon a future. Unlike his contemporaries of the soul music era, however, Brown would maintain an authority in future electronic dance musics and the emergence of minor genres – from Afrobeat to hip-hop – to a degree not readily enjoyed by his peers.

A New Perspective

Even though it does try to make sense of some of the most important events of Brown's musical life, this book is not a biography. Rather, its concern lies with how Brown's musical legacy continues to prevail in such a vital way. One of the major preoccupations of this book is to restore the vitality of Brown's music as an essential ingredient in contemporary dance music aesthetics, and to provide evidence of how his work would help to "produce" unforeseen future musical syntheses. In this respect, historically inclined perspectives do not really tell us anything about why the refrains of James Brown continue to "work." A true appraisal of James Brown should make sense of the vast and disparate musical connections that have been forged in his name, connections that have inspired a creative evolution of electronic dance music and an influence ubiquitous within the contemporary soundscape. For rather than simply name check him amongst a litany of artists responsible for electronic dance music, as in the many other books I have surveyed in this chapter, what is required is an *ontology*, or an explanation for the vitality of Brown's music, and funk in particular, that will more actively account for his emphatic assault on popular music's harnessing of time.

The claim of this book is that the emergence of Brown's funk, commonly dated to the 1965 release of 'Papa's Got a Brand New Bag', and appearing at the very peak of civil-rights optimism, was simply more than just mere coincidence. Despite the wealth of critical attention "the one" has received over the years, one of the most glaring oversights of the literature is the lack of attention paid to the historical *timing* of its appearance in Brown's oeuvre. The propulsive drive of funk, charged as it was with the dynamism of the civil-rights era, constitutes an aesthetic reflection of broader existential conditions which Brown would, in turn, "render musical." The genesis of this idea derives from the work of French philosophers, Gilles Deleuze and Félix Guattari, who contend that it is the role of the artist to "render visible" rather than render or reproduce that which is already visible (Deleuze and Guattari 1988: 342):

> the painter does "not render the visible, but renders visible"; implied here are forces that are not visible, and for a musician, it's the same thing: the musician does not render the audible, he/she renders audible forces that are not audible, making audible the music of the earth, music in which he/she invents, exactly like the philosopher (Deleuze and Parnet 1996).

In their account of what the musical composition might "render visible," Deleuze and Guattari write, "music molecularizes sound matter and in so doing becomes capable of harnessing such nonsonorous forces as Duration and Intensity" (Deleuze and Guattari 1988: 343).

This book attempts an application of this idea, arguing that Brown would harness some of these many immanent, "nonsonorous forces" that existed around him and re-channel them into the radical new musical aesthetic of funk; and that his musical achievement was ultimately predicated on his ability to have "rendered visible" the inner life of the "minority" subject, to "apprehend a minor temporality" and constitute it as a musical form.

While a more involved qualification of this term will be explored throughout the book, for present purposes, the concept might be simply understood as a counter-hegemonic expression of time, where funk would capture a "feeling" of the "minority" and reflect that into a form of musical expression. Through the release of singles such as 'Papa's Got a Brand New Bag' (1965) and 'Cold Sweat' (1967), Brown's decisive rhythmic shift should be considered contextually, as a process of grappling with immanent political forces, rather than emerging as a product of deliberate calculation. As he explains in reference to the release of 'Papa's Got a Brand New Bag': 'It's a little beyond me right now . . . I can't really understand it. It's the only thing on the market that sounds like it. It's different. It's a new bag, just like I sang' (Weinger and Leeds 1996).

This book proposes that the funk aesthetic must constitute a musical aggregate of broader social forces, an "apprehension of a minor temporality," or a reflection of minority existence rendered musical. This ontology of funk is an existential framework in which to understand how certain forms of expression, such as the music of James Brown, might catalyse the experience of African-Americans and allow them to move into the future differently.

Apprehension of a Minor Temporality

This exploration of funk's musical and philosophical legacy is imbued with the philosophy of Deleuze and Guattari. There is a good reason for this. The work of these philosophers is particularly complementary to an aesthetic analysis driven by art's "mode of constitution," that is to say, not by what a work might "mean" but rather how it "works" (Deleuze and Guattari 1983: 109). In this respect, Brown's music provides an enticing example for such analysis due indeed to its enduring capacity to "work." Funk not only offered a valuable musical articulation of immanent circumstance, but would also live on and animate unforeseen musical connections decades into the future. In this respect, this book posits the "apprehension of a minor temporality" as an ontological, rather than significative, analysis of Brown's work, turning instead to funk's mode of constitution, or perhaps more generally the "forces" that drove its creation. As Deleuze and Guattari have argued, the power of art derives not from what it attempts to represent but is driven, instead, by the affective power of sensation, as explained here by Daniel W. Smith:

> Properly speaking there is no "theory of art" in Deleuze . . . each of the arts, and each work of art, confronts its own particular problems, utilising its own particular material and techniques, and attempting to capture intensive forces of very diverse types. To say that the aim of art is not to represent the world, but to present a sensation (which is itself a composition of forces, an intensive synthesis of differential relations), is to say that every sensation, ever work of art is *singular*, and that the conditions of sensation are at the same time the conditions for the production of the *new* (Smith 1996: 41).

This shift from a preoccupation with art's representative function, to a commitment to the uncovering of forces that are catalysed in the artwork, requires an "affective" perspective, one somewhat at odds, perhaps, with the traditional biographical emphasis on a presentation of historical "facts." For when it comes to qualifying Brown's invention, "the facts" do not necessarily elucidate the forces that might have inspired him to create in the first place. If James Brown "invented" "the one," then surely we must extend our interests to examining what fostered such a concept, and what underlying historical circumstances may have contributed to its emergence? Proposing an answer to this question requires an evaluation of how art "works," and how it renders immanent forces into artistic composition.

Art and Affect

Art, according to Deleuze and Guattari, is properly concerned with the creation of percepts and affects, which work together to constitute "a bloc of sensations" (Deleuze and Guattari 1994: 164). As the philosophers have argued, it is this production of sensation, rather than representation, that is truly the domain of creative art. That is to say, our attempts to make "sense" of art through representation, and to imbue it with our own subjective "meaning," simply undermines the more important concern of how the work of art *affects*, or how it intervenes in, the relationship between bodies. In service of this non-representational approach to art, the philosophers argue that "the work of art is a being of sensation and nothing else: it exists in itself" (Deleuze and Guattari 1994: 164). For Deleuze and Guattari, art has no ultimate meaning; it exists as a catalyst of affective sensation, where these "affects *are* becomings" (Deleuze and Guattari 1988: 256), that is, the catalysts of change, both corporeal and incorporeal, in material bodies. Thus what is at issue in this book is the impact of Brown's music in fostering the affective encounter, and how such encounters have, quite simply, effected ongoing social and political change. This book will argue that it is through affect that Brown recreates a possibility for belief in the world via a promotion of connections between thought and the affective, where such affects – as becomings – are mobilized into social possibilities.

It is true that any creative act is distinguished by its production of affects, yet these affects will always come up against social limitations, or, rather, be framed by those limitations. The task of a more radical work of art is to re-activate affect, outside of "the frame." Distinguishing these affective relations is the basis of the Deleuze-Guattarian concept of ethology: a "practical science of the manners of being. The manner of being is precisely the state of beings (étants), of what exists (existants), from the point of view of a pure ontology" (Deleuze 1998). What concerns us here is the instigation of new affective relations that might, in turn, constitute a more immanent form of politics. This micro-political process is based around experimenting with the capacities of a body as it might affect new relations upon the world; relations that may hopefully move beyond those imposed by a "common sense" image of thought. The artist, which includes Brown himself, will have to mediate at this important juncture between unrestrained affective possibility and "common sense." It is the artist who is sufficiently naïve to make the attempt to overturn the majoritarian *representation* of events, and it is through their art that a minor politics is given affective substance.

This is not always a completely intentional process on the part of the artist. In the case of Brown, his approach to music *becomes* political through its accommodation of new bodily expressions that will ultimately extend into alternative means for thought. This "empiricist conversion" begins with a "belief in the body," and is central to Deleuze's contention that a belief in the world is a belief in the body itself (Deleuze 1989: 172). To understand what Deleuze means by "a body" here, I am referring to a non-referential sense of the body rather than being a body *of something*, for instance, a predetermined, gendered or racialized body. Becoming, then, might result from attempts to make that body work for itself rather than simply beholden to the terms of its representation. Through a belief in the world (and body) we might be able to connect people with the world again, and perhaps restore the artificial divisions that we have created between the body and the "outside" (Deleuze 1989: 172). From here we might begin to more readily embrace the unpredictable results that will undoubtedly ensue:

> We know nothing about a body until we know what it can do, in other words, what its affects are, how they can or cannot enter into composition with other affects, with the affects of another body, either to destroy that body or to be destroyed by it, either to exchange actions or passions with it or to join with it in composing a more powerful body (Deleuze and Guattari 1988: 257).

If any performer is synonymous with pushing the boundaries of what a body could do, it is James Brown. This is an assessment based not only on the intensity of Brown's dance routines and performances, but also as a reflection of his idiosyncratic approach to musical expression. Approaching Brown's legacy this way may appear to be precariously headed up some essentialist path, a conferring of "blackness" as synonymous with the "body." This is most certainly not the case, although it is true that the specificity of bodies matters. For a start, the question is one of the body as always the mediator of affects and, as such, of what the body can contribute to thought. That which moves the body is direct and immediate, and Brown's music is superlative in this sense as it implores us to engage with the site of affect. It is in this pursuit of affect that we might more readily understand the ongoing popularity of Brown's refrains. In many forms of contemporary electronic music, the Brown sample works within the musical composition as a catalysing agent and thus gives expression to its imminent social environment. When James Brown's music is re-presented as sample, it no longer signifies solely on the level of a representation of "James Brown," but rather constitutes part of a new expression of a "becoming music." Excised from their original context, a sample of a scream, a yell, or a funky drummer beat provides an affective catalyst that facilitates a new and unforeseen textual relationship. That

Brown's music has been sampled so very much, is ultimately due this superlative capacity to affect, which translates into dynamic territorialization.

Of course we need to examine further the primacy of affect to all bodies. In the translator's preface to *A Thousand Plateaus*, Brian Massumi, after Deleuze and Guattari, explains affect in the following way:

> Affect/Affection. Neither word denotes a personal feeling ... *L'affect* (Spinoza's *affectus*) is an ability to affect and be affected. It is a prepersonal intensity corresponding to the passage from one experiential state of the body to another and implying an augmentation or diminution of that body's capacity to act (Massumi in Deleuze and Guattari 1988: xvi).

In short, the Deleuzean concept of affect should not be merely conflated with a general understanding of emotion, which is generally the linguistic product of affective encounter. This foregrounds the problem of a lack of "cultural-theoretical vocabulary specific to affect. Our entire vocabulary has derived from theories of signification that are still wedded to structure even across irreconcilable differences ... In the absence of an asignifying philosophy of affect, it is all too easy for received psychological categories to slip back in, undoing the considerable deconstructive work that has been effectively carried out by poststructuralism" (Massumi 1996: 221). To restore the primacy of affect in the encounter between bodies, we must always ask, "not what it means, but how does it work?"

Cinema Books

Alleviating affect from subjectification and signification are central tenets of Deleuze's *Cinema 1: The Movement-Image* (1983) and *Cinema 2: The Time-Image* (1989) both of which are deployed to analyse Brown's work in this book. While utilizing cinematic theory to explain musical composition may initially appear a strange proposition, Deleuze's *Cinema* books provide a broader and more general schematic of aesthetic change, presenting philosophical concepts that can be deployed beyond their immediate cinematic context. My own pursuit of funk's temporal constitution as one reflecting broader existential circumstances is inspired by Deleuze's deliberate move away from "reading" certain films, to broach instead their particular mode of constitution.

A Musical Future 25

In short, Brown's funk groove might best be discussed as an aesthetic response to the existential conditions that grew out of the often perceived "failure" of the civil-rights movement in the 1960s, where teleological collapse facilitates an aesthetic that eschews a more hegemonic, "common sense," composition of time and space. If the concern of the *Cinema* books is to illustrate the shift from the depiction of movement through time (the "movement-image") to a more direct experience of the temporal (the "time-image"), exacerbated by the intolerable events of World War II, then the transitional period of this book is leveraged instead upon the apparent decline of the civil-rights era.

As the optimism of the soul era makes way for the cynicism of post-soul, the more linear conventions of traditional narrative and telos make way for a reality of temporal indeterminacy. As funk and electronic dance musics reflect the experiential time of "minorities" rendered musical, these styles might exhibit a "time-image" eschewal of a narratively driven, "common sense" view of historical time, more pertinent to the imminent existential conditions of their emergence. As such, funk is an aesthetic strategy that constitutes a "minor temporality."

The conceptual framework used to mobilize and make sense of this apprehension of a "minor temporality" reflects the schematic approach of Deleuze's *Cinema* books, in that it attempts to make sense of changes in the relation of "images of thought" (more later) to time, where an emphasis from the narratives of soul gives way to a more indeterminate, less hegemonically defined sense of time, one that emerges in the "irrational," non-linearity of the funk composition. In this respect, Brown's music presents itself as a source of becoming for a minority population that was denied this capacity in the broader macropolitical world.

Whether framing the existential circumstances of his own context of composition, or of the continuing influence he has on a future of music, the best approach toward evaluating Brown's musical legacy is, of course, in those connections made by, and through, his music. Brown's ongoing influence as an ontological force is a far more vital proposition than textual analysis might afford. Here we are attempting to deal with Brown as a figure of transformational creative capacity, of an affectivity that entices an ongoing engagement with his music, not just from the point of view of a general audience, but via those DJs and "crate diggers" who use Brown's body of work as no less than a library of virtual musical possibility. The success of Brown's work lay in its ability to keep on connecting, and it is this force of connection, *affect*, which is at the heart of this productivity. Thus efforts to translate Brown's affectivity into the discursive, perhaps a formalist response to his musical compositions, is ultimately an exercise in futility, for as Félix Guattari points out, "affect is not a question of representation and discursivity, but of existence" (Guattari 1995: 93):

> They start to exist in you, in spite of you. And not only as crude, undifferentiated affects, but as hyper-complex compositions: that's Debussy, that's Jazz, that's Van Gogh. The paradox which aesthetic experience constantly returns us to is that these affects, as a mode of existential apprehension, are given all at once, regardless, or besides the fact that indicative traits and descriptive refrains are necessary for catalysing their existence in fields of representation (Guattari 1995: 93).

This idea of affect as "a mode of existential apprehension" encompasses a capacity beyond signification. Indeed, music often works *in spite* of its nominal signification. In his essay, "Signifying Nothing: 'Culture', 'Discourse' and the Sociality of Affect" (2004), Jeremy Gilbert argues for an affective based theory of music, one that might diverge from the more significationally dependent musicological analysis:

> Music has physical effects which can be identified, described and discussed but which are not the same thing as it having meanings, and any attempt to understand how music works in culture must, as many commentators over the years have acknowledged, be able to say something about those effects without trying to collapse them into meanings (Gilbert 2004b).

Gilbert provides the example of the hip-hop artist, whose criticisms of white culture are so enthusiastically embraced by that very same demographic. As poststructuralism has already told us, the reduction of a text to a universal "meaning" is a futile endeavour, as they will only ever be subjective. In fact, the fundamental function of music is not merely one of signification anyway:

> The problem we have is that music is by definition an organised form of experience, one whose effectivity is strictly delimited by sedimented cultural practices, but it is one whose structured effects cannot be fully understood in terms of meanings; precisely, they cannot be understood according to the structural logic of language. It is to this point that I think this set of reflections leads us – to the observation that, at least as far as music is concerned, a notion of "culture" which sees in it only "signifying practices" is quite simply not up to the job. Music is obviously cultural, but its "culturality" is not limited to its capacity to signify (Gilbert 2004b).

Which leads music writer, Simon Reynolds, a committed fan of Deleuze and Guattari himself, to enquire whether commentary on affectively driven dance music cultures should eschew signification completely, or if "it [is] possible to base a culture around sensations rather than truths, fascination rather than meaning?" (Reynolds 1999: 10).

While this enquiry will be taken further through the course of this book, one of the most pertinent observations to be made at this juncture is that art should never be fixed down to notions of intent; that it can only seek an audience, or seek a people. The power of affect can never be simply reduced to signification, nor to language. In fact, one of the main concerns of Deleuze and Guattari's philosophy is to dispel the notion that language structures conscious and unconscious life, to emphasize instead the powers of the affective that might constitute desire and its manifestation as artistic intent. The imperative of art is to communicate the intensity of feeling that generally escapes articulation, or the attempts to express those parts of existence that language cannot adequately describe. This is why I have argued for the Deleuze-Guattarian approach, where the work of art is designed to plunge its audience into a becoming, rather than merely reiterate what could otherwise be simply expressed in language. In short, language is inadequate to the task of translating the full power of affect, which is how funk transpires in the first place, as a tangible musical expression, or the "rendering visible" of the affect of the civil-rights movement.

Which is why Deleuze will argue, in *Cinema 1*, that cinema should not be read at a level of narrative, such as that espoused by a structuralist, psychoanalytic reading of film, but should move away from representation completely. While Deleuze acknowledges that the cinema initially took on the human perspective as a purveyor of "meaning" via a system of action – "the movement-image" – the medium eventually drops this filter of signification and "becomes" a revelation of time itself. The regimes of movement-image and time-image always co-exist, however they can be seen to predominate at certain stages, those that reflect a particular social and collective psyche or what we will later describe as the "spiritual automaton."

The "spiritual automaton" is a proclivity towards a new way of thinking, the result of something in the world that forces us to think. As it is discussed in terms of the *Cinema* books, this accompanying change in thinking and existential orientation was irrevocably affected by the events of World War II. While this has much in common with other poststructuralist and postmodernist philosophy, Deleuze's position differs somewhat from the commentary of his "postmodern" peers in the sense that this nominal break doesn't lead to a decline in the loss of the real, but proposes instead a renewed relation to the affective. For Deleuze affect is always immanent. Indeed, as affects mobilize the universe, they cannot simply wane; rather it is just a matter of modulation and relativity. The evolution of any art form can be perceived as such a series of affective machinic relations, and in this respect a history of contemporary dance music quite clearly presents to us a history of such affects as the mediation between bodies. Hence we should be concerned with what the medium tells us about the context in which we are living or the mode of enunciation of that medium. This should be understood as the expression of affective relations rather than significative ones, which is where the utility of music comes into its own, as an affective mediator.

Using resources such as the work of Gilles Deleuze, among others, this book attempts to qualify how aesthetic change in musical "composition," such as that exhibited by the transformations in Brown's work, might reflect a shift in "mental" orientation, driven by the immanent political climate. In common with Deleuze's *Cinema* books which inspired this type of ontology, this book gives special attention to the role of the temporal in transforming the capacity to think, and, in turn, create.

Becoming and Time

Music is time, and musical innovations, such as funk, provide us with new perspectives on time, and, by extension, new creative capacities for thought. Framing the construction of funk as an "apprehension of a minor temporality" is to extrapolate how music might render visible the temporality of lived experience, that form of time proposed by Henri Bergson as *durée*, "whose reality is an indivisible, ceaseless, and ever-changing flow" (Rodowick 1997: 122). The attempts to render visible this experience of *durée* has conceptual precedents in other fields of artistic work, such as the aforementioned cinematic example, or the influence of Bergson's *durée* in early twentieth-century novels. In *Bergson and the Stream of Consciousness Novel* (1962), Shiv Kumar analysed how the flow of time central to Bergsonian duration would influence the emergence of the "stream of consciousness" style of authors such as Dorothy Richardson, James Joyce and Virginia Woolf whose work embraced Bergsonian philosophy of the early twentieth century. These authors moved away from depicting narrative as chronological time, to capture the experience of experiential flow of *durée*. This time as duration can be more simply understood as the subjective experience of time – a less simple, less linear experience of time. For example, a ride in the bus that takes 40 minutes in chronological, or "clock time," might seem considerably longer (or shorter) in terms of lived durational experience. The "stream of consciousness" approach emerged as a method of bringing the expression of the transcendental *durée* to the fore. For instance, instead of describing the action of characters as occurring within a universalized notion of linear time and fixed space, the "stream of consciousness" style would instead emphasize the explorations of the composition of time to the point where it obscured the more predetermined time/space of the traditional narrative form. As Kumar has argued, this "stream of consciousness" approach would capitalize upon Bergson's revised perspective on time (Kumar 1962: 5–10), and foreground a revised existential time in the process.

We could look to the artistic depiction of the unfolding, lived experience of time as illustrated by these "stream of consciousness" authors, as an interesting foundation for a revised perspective of understanding Brown's funk; a method of analysis that attempts to divulge the broader existential forces that lay behind aesthetic change. Within the context of Brown's music, we might think of the shift in rhythm instigated by Brown through his concept of "the one," as a new apprehension – or capture – of time. From there we can begin to ask ourselves, what may have inspired this commitment to the production of a new musical time, and what might the impetus have been?

In short, this book argues that Brown's funk acts as an important aesthetic intermediary for making sense of the changes in existential time that defined the "soul" and "post-soul" eras. While a more nuanced extrapolation of these periods, and Brown's role in their composition, will follow, what might be understood at this early stage is that Brown's funk was prescient of the existential shift away from the collective euphoria of that civil-rights era soul period, and into the post-1968, post-King, "post-soul" era. Brown's radical musical decisions in the mid-1960s would drive his musical divergence from the more orthodox compositional styles of popular soul and into the repetitive funk groove, where the non-teleological repetition of the funk style beckons the shift away from the linear progress inherent to the narratives of the soul aesthetic.

Thus for a decade spanning the mid-1960s to mid-1970s, arguably Brown's most artistically accomplished, he would "prepare" modern music for radical change by harnessing compositional aesthetics that would reflect the broader existential/ontological concerns of these respective eras. In the process he would enable a future of new music styles in turn, and he would provide for this future by imploring "a people to come" (Deleuze and Guattari 1988: 345). The role of the artist, according to Deleuze, is not simply concerned with, "addressing a people, which is presupposed already there, but of contributing to the invention of a people" (Deleuze 1989: 217).

Brown's "people to come" might be observed among those generations that had to live life in the wake of the soul era, which in the work of Nelson George and Mark Anthony Neal has been conceptualized as the "post-soul" generation. This is a generation whose aesthetic values are marked by their indignant perspective of the soul years. For, unlike their forebears, this generation was bereft of the promises of social change and would instead have to contend with a state of existential disarray. Despite this being an "intolerable" state of affairs, it would of course stimulate aesthetic change; a change that I believe would be reflected in a new compositional orientation to time, and one that it would be impossible to conceive of, without Brown's intervention.

2 The Early Years

The drive and propulsion that would characterize funk is part and parcel of the very life force that transformed Brown's lonely and impoverished childhood into one of popular music's greatest success stories. Entering the world in the midst of the Depression into the heavily segregated Deep South of Barnwell, South Carolina in 1933, Brown was immediately inculcated into a life of struggle. Fighting from his very first moments, the infant Brown entered the world as a stillborn, surviving only through the tenacious resuscitative efforts of an aunt. His subsequent childhood years brought little further relief; the boy was abandoned by his mother at the age of two, and, given the precarious employment conditions of the time, eventually by his father too. Placed in the care of yet another aunt, the proprietor of a brothel in Augusta's "Terry" – a contraction of "Negro territory" – it was in this rather less-than-wholesome environment that the juvenile Brown pursued a series of novel enterprises to earn his keep.

As recounted in Adrian Maben's rarely seen, *Soul Brother No. 1* (1978), Brown's childhood was preoccupied with survival. The boy attempted to contribute to the household income by shining shoes, collecting bottles, stamps, and "clinkers" (twice-burnt coal) to keep warm, and generally hustling where he could. Brown would also become adept at soliciting on behalf of his aunt's establishment, performing "buck dances" for a clientele that included the troops of nearby Camp Gordon whose convoys would serendipitously pass Aunt Honey's business on their way to base. With the young man's independence also came solitude, and his loneliness was kept at bay through music, via a harmonica gifted by his father, or some rudimentary guitar taught to him by no less than bluesman Tampa Red, who also frequented Aunt Honey's establishment.

Given that such necessary material pursuits would inevitably impede on his formal education, Brown's vocational outlook was rather restricted, and his survival was somewhat understandably unencumbered by the bounds of the law. The troubled youth would eventually wind up serving time at the age of sixteen, charged with several counts of breaking and entering automobiles.

On June 13, 1949, the barely sixteen-year-old Brown was sentenced eight to sixteen years for his transgression, and packed off to the Georgia Juvenile Training Institute in Rome, Georgia, to duly serve his time. While the conditions of the incarceration could have been worse, as Brown recounts in his 1986 autobiography, the Juvenile Training Institute "was more like a school than a tough prison" (Brown and Tucker 1986: 37). If anything it was certain to have been a bewildering experience for the teenager, even more so, when, after serving the first two years, Brown, along with the rest of the inmates, was moved to Camp Toccoa, a former paratrooper base.

Rather than harbouring resentment about these tumultuous early years, Brown has always remained sanguine about the experience, if only because prison provided him with his first opportunities to display his musical capabilities to a wider audience. Camp Toccoa would, at least, provide access to a common-room piano and regular choir practice, and Brown soon earned his reputation as a gifted vocalist.

Fiercely competitive by nature, "Music Box," as he came to be known among the inmates, gave his all to each and every endeavour, and his sporting prowess was just as renowned as his musical ability. It was in service of the former, rather than the latter, that brought Brown into contact with the man who would become an integral musical ally, Bobby Byrd. Byrd was a member of a local baseball team who had come to play against the inmates of the Georgia Boys Industrial Institute, as Camp Toccoa was now known. In the midst of play, Brown and Byrd struck up a conversation (Hay 2003: 113) based on the brief Byrd had received from the inmates during a previous visit. A fledgling musician himself, Byrd's interest was piqued. Now standing before him in the flesh, "Music Box" impressed upon Byrd his personal situation, explaining that he could secure release if only he could find an employer to sponsor him. Sufficiently impressed by the boy's plight, Byrd lobbied his family for assistance.

Thanks to the efforts of Bobby and his family, who petitioned the governor of the Institute for Brown's release, Brown left Camp Toccoa in June 1952. During this time the popularity of "rhythm and blues" was in full bloom. A genre spurred on by a preponderance of small black music labels that emerged during the burgeoning prosperity of the post-war period, some of the R&B performers who inspired Brown included such luminaries as Louis Jordan, the jump-blues wailers Roy Brown and Wynonie Harris, and vocal groups such as The Dominoes, The "5" Royales and Hank Ballard and The Midnighters.

The impact of these R&B influences are discussed in the liner notes to the album *Messing with the Blues* (1990), penned by Brown expert and confidante, Cliff White, for whom Brown reflects upon these formative years:

> No one inspired me more than Louis Jordan and Roy Brown. Jordan was just an unbelievable performer, writer, arranger, actor. And a businessman, too ... But Roy Brown had the dynamics. That's the main reason I was able to sing hard, because I emulated him when I first started. I got the power and the drive from him, and combined it with my gospel background. That's where the soul comes from (Brown in White 1990).

While central to the repertoire of Bobby Byrd's group, The Avons (also known as the Gospel Starlighters in their sacred incarnation), the music of these R&B performers was not nearly an enticing enough proposition for Brown at this early stage. Declining the invitation to join Bobby's group, Brown seemed to have been rather more interested in the straight gospel of the local community choir, the Ever Ready Gospel Singers, in which Bobby's sister Sarah was a member (G. Brown 1996: 39). The fact that Brown and Sarah Byrd were now "going together" was probably a key factor in the decision, although his commitment to the group's success was paramount.

While the group became popular enough locally to warrant a demo recording at the local Toccoa radio station, WLET, the Ever Ready Gospel Singers failed to gain any real momentum. In the wake of their demise, Brown simply gravitated towards the other Byrd ensemble. While developing many secular tunes with Bobby's group, Brown recounts in his autobiography that he "hadn't given up on gospel entirely" (Brown and Tucker 1986: 37). Indeed, the influence of the gospel composition and its intense repetitive incantation would provide a salient aesthetic consideration evident from Brown's very first release.

Please, Please, Please

After enjoying some measure of local success, the Ever Ready Gospel Singers would enter the Macon, Georgia studio of radio station, WIBB, to cut a demo of a drastically reworked version of the old Blues staple, 'Baby Please Don't Go'. Likely influenced by the 1952 hit for the Orioles, the final product would ultimately bear little resemblance to its predecessor, as 'Please, Please, Please' (1956) that left the studio was utterly reconceptualized. It was a copy of this raw, but intense, demo that would eventually make its way to Ralph Bass, A&R for the Cincinnati-based, King records, whose favourable response provided the Famous Flames (as the group was now known) with their first formal recording session.

Repetitious even by the standards of the rather rudimentary structures of the then emergent rock'n'roll composition, 'Please, Please, Please' is an early testament to Brown's remarkable tenacity in getting a record released at all. As the story goes, Syd Nathan, then boss of King Records, thought so little of his A&R man's latest discovery that Ralph Bass was almost fired when the boss listened to Brown's first disc: "I get Syd on the phone. He's yelling: 'Bass what kind of shit you on?! I don't know what he is talking about. That's the worst piece of shit I've ever heard! He's just singing one word'" (Bass in G. Brown 1996: 56). That Nathan would respond to the Flames' demo with such an extreme reaction is rather curious, considering that the King label housed many other formidable gospel artists on their roster, including Little Willie John, Hank Ballard, and Joe Tex among others. Faced with losing his job over this apparent faux pas, Bass protested with the following challenges to his employer: "I told Syd, 'Don't fire me. Put it out in Atlanta, test it. You'll see'. He says, 'Fuck it! I'm putting it out all across the country, just to prove what a piece of shit it is'" (ibid.) As Douglas Wolk has argued, financially committing to a nationwide release is hardly a typical response of displeasure (Wolk 2004: 75). Whether the tale is apocryphal or not, the reality of the matter was that 'Please, Please, Please' would thoroughly defy Syd Nathan's lowered expectations, and its circulation around the markets of the South would eventually garner enough momentum to provide the Famous Flames with their first million-selling record (White 1989).

Not that this triumph was reflected in the attribution on the record's label. While the Famous Flames went into their premier recording session as a group, the artist credited on the label of 'Please, Please, Please' was now, "*James Brown With* The Famous Flames," as the other Flames had found themselves relegated to the status of backing band. Whether this turn of events was due to the prominence of Brown's lead vocal, or simply an early indication of the singer's capacity to undermine his peers, remains unresolved; suffice to say that the Flames had much to gain by foregrounding Brown's unique vocal talents not least the inextricable torrent of emotional energy that came with Brown's purging of his soul.

On the surface, 'Please, Please, Please' would appear simple to the point of insipid, the phrase "baby please don't go" reiterated in various states of emotional duress, a song lacking any real "development," either lyrically or melodically. Yet it is precisely such idiosyncratic qualities that contribute to its audacious novelty, a modulation of affective states far more significant than its modest lyricism, a point described in the following passage by Philip Gourevitch, as part of his superlative *New Yorker* profile, "Mr. Brown: On the Road with his Bad Self":

> The song doesn't tell a story so much as express a condition. The singer might be speaking from the cradle of his lover's arms or chasing her down a street, or watching the lights of her train diminish in the night; he might be crouched alone in an alleyway, or wandering an empty house, or smiling for all the world to see while his words rattle, unspoken, inside his skull. He could be anyone anywhere. His lover might be dying. He might be dying. He might not even be addressing an actual lover. He could be speaking of someone or something he's never had. He could be talking to God, or to the Devil. It doesn't matter. Despite the implication of a story, a specific predicament, the song is abstract. The words jockey for release and describe the impossibility of release, yet the singing is pure release, defiant, exultant. Speech is inadequate, so the singer makes music, and music is inadequate, so he makes his music speak. Feeling is snipped to its essence, and the feeling is the whole story. And, if that feeling seems inelegant, the singer's immaculately disciplined performance makes his representation of turmoil unmistakably styled and stylish – the brink of frenzy as a style unto itself (Gourevitch 2002: 48).

Gospel

The success of 'Please, Please, Please' was leveraged upon the increasing commercial success of gospel, which continued to flourish in the post-war period. While the roots of gospel can be traced back to the eighteenth century, the birth of modern gospel is attributed to the year 1930, when the National Baptist Convention first publicly endorsed the compositions of Professor Thomas Dorsey. Operating out of Chicago from the late 1920s, Dorsey would play an inordinate role in the mainstream recognition of gospel. His establishment of a gospel publishing house aided the development of some of the most promising gospel artists of the time, including that of an up-and-coming Mahalia Jackson, as well as providing an important outlet for Dorsey's new-found preoccupation with sacred composition. His commitment began with "Take My Hand, Precious Lord" which he composed after his wife died in childbirth in 1932. Shaken by this cruel event, Dorsey would turn his back on a burgeoning career in secular composition to concentrate instead on a more sacred style of music – a rather ironic turn of events given that Dorsey's former musical life was notable for its often salacious content. Formerly a blues singer and piano player who went by the stage name of "Georgia Tom," Dorsey was famed for partnerships with blues legends such as Ma Rainey and Brown's esteemed former guitar tutor, Tampa Red (LeRoi Jones 1967: 192):

> In the twenties, Dorsey made a decent living as sideman, writer, and performer. Before he penned gospel classics like "Precious Lord," he wrote double entendre blues titled "It's Tight Like That." In the beginning of his gospel career, his bluesy leanings sometimes got him thrown out of some churches (Hirshey 1985: 27).

The uplifting gospel sounds arrived in time to provide a necessary musical buffer to the Great Depression of the 1930s. While Dorsey had been writing gospel a lot earlier than this, it was in this time of struggle that the music found its true calling: "We tried the gospel songs in the twenties," [Dorsey] said, "but the time was not ripe for it. In the Depression, the time was ripe. People wanted to turn to something. The time is right for what these young fellows are trying to do. It's the age, the Atomic Age. People are scared. They want something to turn to. They're ready for it" (Dorsey in Hirshey 1985: 27). While the commercial potential of recorded gospel was evident as far back as the late 1930s when the guitar-slinging Sister Rosetta Tharpe had a hit with the Dorsey-composed, *Rock Me*, the hits were isolated. It was not until the forties, and perhaps even after the Second World War, that gospel groups and singers would tour major auditoriums, and performers such as Marion Williams, Sallie Martin and Willie Mae Ford Smith would enjoy wider acceptance.

If the Depression helped to birth gospel, then a new set of trying circumstances would help to establish its mainstream tenure. The music found its calling as the soundtrack to a burgeoning civil-rights struggle with Mahalia Jackson its spiritual figurehead. As Amiri Baraka (then writing as LeRoi Jones) argues in his oft-cited essay "The Changing Same (R&B and New Black Music)" (1966), working-class African-Americans had a stronger connection to Gospel as "[it] was the more emotional blacker churches that the blues people were members of, rather than the usually whiter, more middle-class churches the jazz people went to" (LeRoi Jones 1967: 192). Arising from this situation was a rather ironic turn of events whereby, "the gospel singers . . . always had a more direct connection with the blues than the other religious singers" (LeRoi Jones 1967: 192), echoing indeed the personal circumstance of Dorsey himself. The essence of the bond between blues and gospel was an expression of their rootsy, egalitarian appeal:

> Outraged by the growth of classical-oriented jazz and inspired by the success of artists like Mahalia Jackson and Ray Charles, the young New York musicians began in the late Fifties to reassess the Negro folk idiom – the cries, chants, shouts, work songs and pulsating rhythmic vitality of gospel singers and shouting choirs. Then, in one of the most astounding about-faces in jazz history, the fundamentalists (most of them are conservatory-trained liberals) abandoned Bartok, Schoenberg, and "all that jazz" and immersed themselves in the music of Thomas A. Dorsey, Roberta Martin (gospel artists) and Howlin' Wolf. Jazz, which had been rolling along on a fugue kick, turned from the academy and faced the store front church (Bennett in Hirshey 1985: 76).

The timing of this return to "roots" by the decidedly more middle-class jazz fraternity was undoubtedly inspired by the burgeoning political environment, as civil-rights activities, which encompassed the goals of "a people," implored a more inclusive soundtrack. The embrace of gospel, channelled into the musical activities of the soul jazz artists of the time, was a harnessing of the power of an already inextricable ingredient in the lives of many African-Americans. Its inspiration was undoubtedly its status as a catalysing agent, a musical conduit that might, at this crucial time, inspire this "minor" people into a collective.

The 'Minor'

Introduced previously as constituent of the notion of a "minor temporality," the concept of the "minor" requires some further elucidation. Derived from Deleuze and Guattari's book, *Kafka: Toward a Minor Literature* (1986) and elaborated in their subsequent works, most notably *A Thousand Plateaus* (1988), the minor is not an identification, nor can it be represented as such, but is, instead, a "becoming," a position held by those opposed to the majoritarian or dominant forces of social "stratification." Quite simply, if the majoritarian is a conformity to the general state of things, then the minority is becoming something else. The differences between the two can perhaps be understood in the following way: the purpose of the majoritarian is to maintain stasis via common sense, similitude, habit, banality and pretty much all of the other methods of maintaining the apparent stability of everyday life. The majoritarian culture must, by nature, embrace conformity as it tries to keep bodies moving in a given space rather than allowing a shifting space to move through changing bodies.

The minor, then, can be perceived as the escape route from the dominant culture. In this sense, given that life is change, the minor culture is always better oriented to embrace this change compared to its major counterpart. Deleuze and Guattari have summarized these opposing orientations in the following way: "we must distinguish between the majoritarian as a constant and homogeneous system; minorities as subsystems; and the minoritarian as a potential, creative and created, becoming" (Deleuze and Guattari 1988: 105–106). This Deleuze-Guattarian concept of minority should necessarily be differentiated from its more common understanding, and, as such, the categories of major and minor are not simply understood in quantitative terms, but instead as reflections of relative power. As Deleuze writes here:

> The difference between minorities and majorities isn't their size. A minority may be bigger than a majority. What defines the majority is a model you have to conform to: the average European adult male city-dweller, for example . . . A minority, on the other hand, has no model, it's a becoming, a process. One might say the majority is nobody. Everybody's caught,

one way or another, in a minority becoming that would lead them into unknown paths if they opted to follow it through. When a minority creates models for itself, it's because it wants to become a majority, and probably has to, to survive or prosper (to have a state, be recognized, establish its rights, for example). But its power comes from what it's managed to create, which to some extent goes into the model, but doesn't depend on it: A people is always a creative minority, and remains one even when it acquires a majority: it can be both at once, because the two things aren't lived out on the same plane (Deleuze 1995: 173–74).

By way of illustration, Deleuze and Guattari employ the work of Franz Kafka, as exemplary of a "minor" literature. They explain how Kafka, as a Czech Jew, would express his minority by assuming a writing style that would utilize a variety of languages – the Czech vernacular, Hebrew (what Deleuze and Guattari refer to as the mythic language), Yiddish, which itself is a "nomadic movement of deterritorialization that reworks German" (Deleuze and Guattari 1986: 25), as well as the literature of his milieu, Prague German. Prague German itself, Deleuze and Guattari add, "is a deterritorialized language, appropriate for strange and minor uses. (This can be compared in another context to what blacks in America today are able to do with the English language)" (Deleuze and Guattari 1986: 17). The minor literature of Kafka or Afro-American vernacular is a becoming, in the sense that it creates its way out of the strictures of linguistic domination in the majoritarian culture from which it transpires. Extricated from the majority, and with little capacity to constitute it, this precarious situation beckons a creativity of survival, where the minor is forced into creation as a way of life; which is why the "minor literature," while working within a major language, will always remain apart from it. This marginality forces the minor author to become "a sort of stranger within his own language" (Deleuze and Guattari 1986: 26) making use, as it does, of a plurilingualism reflective of the writer's schizophrenic environmental assemblage. Yet this plurilingualism is ultimately beneficial as it provides the minor with a "revolutionary force" pushing "deterritorialization to such an extreme that nothing remains but intensities" (Deleuze and Guattari 1986: 19). As a product of displacement, and a creative response to a lack of identity, the minor literature is not the product of an individual subject, but rather a collective enunciation of "a people" and an expression of a "revolutionary machine-to-come" (Deleuze and Guattari 1986: 18). The form of this revolutionary machine-to-come is manifest "as seeds, crystals of becoming whose value is to trigger uncontrollable movements and deterritorializations of the mean or majority" (Deleuze and Guattari 1988: 106).

While we still have some way to go before the historical moment of Brown's funk, the fact that Brown himself was deterritorializing the gospel tradition, and transforming it, or reterritorializing it in his own inimitable way, provides for this capacity of minor musical creation. Brown's music, which reaches its apotheosis in funk, reflects as musical composition the *becoming* of Afro-America, where the shift in rhythmic emphasis to "the one" constitutes a similar capture of intensities that might be found in Kafka's minor literature. In the case of James Brown, his revolutionary contribution was manifest in a re-assembly of duration in a way that, through its appeals to dance and or bodily presence, would allow for new and increasingly radical affective relations and associations between bodies. That process of territorialization, instigated by Brown's dynamic and beckoning musical force, provides an undeniably important catalyst for a collective becoming.

Later we will see how other minor music makers, such as the hip-hop DJs of some of America's most invisible and impoverished territories, will sample the work of Brown to inform their own minor becoming. We can see how these artistic practices are totally necessary for a population that has no capacity to make territorial claims on the official truths of history, and is thus denied identity because of this. That is why the minor will instead take up what might be perceived as the "false" (from the point of view of "official truth" or "common sense"), an openness to the infinite dimensions of coexistent alterities that might be used to oppose official (and rather more static) versions of history: "history is made only by those who oppose history (not by those who insert themselves into it, or even reshape it)" (Deleuze and Guattari 1988: 295–96).

In this context was can see how the music of James Brown might foster the alterity of minority, further ensuring its popularity among these populations for many years to come. Whether a beat, break, or sample, fragments of Brown's music are the seeds of a newly revised relation to history, a creative capacity of the "powers of the false" and central to the establishment of the longevity of Brown's minority position. For his unyielding relationship to a "black" musical aesthetic, the embrace of repetition, Brown's minority would be ensured.

Repetition as a Figure of Black Culture

Even if "the one" was yet to be formally instated as a musical concept, the release of 'Please, Please, Please' offered an enduring constitutive element of Brown's musical sensibility. In an interview in *Uncut* (2004) magazine, Brown would directly attribute gospel as the very source of "the one": "Gospel always had The One," Brown says, "but it became more dominant once I clarified it" (Brown in Hoskyns 2004: 68). His predilection for incessant, repetitive incantation, of often a single phrase, was not only significant of his musical aesthetic, but more importantly, the cyclical nature of this repetition indicates a wholly different relationship to time. As Cynthia Rose writes:

> Brown's repetition and circularity – clearly transferred from sacred to secular musics and performance – are something much larger than a personal eccentricity. They denote a black culture with Afrocentric values, values distinctly separate from white European systems of thought about the physical world . . . The Afrocentric world view to which repetitions like James Brown's allude, then, consciously or as received patterns, is not one of linear progression (Rose 1990: 121).

The Afrocentric values to which Rose refers are discussed in detail in James A. Snead's seminal essay, "Repetition as a Figure of Black Culture" (1998 [1981]). As Snead contends in that piece, repetition has been misunderstood and subsequently undermined in European culture (Snead 1998: 67–69), and this misunderstanding of black and white approaches to the temporal comes to a head in black popular music. Snead argues that the repetition inherent not only to black music, but to black culture in general, reflects a compositional value concerned with *circulation* (1998: 69), an aesthetic much in distinction to the compositional values of *accumulation and growth* (ibid.), and central to the values of a European sensibility marked by a concern with building the composition into a more regulated compositional "totality." At the heart of European composition is the teleological "goal" and just as "in European culture, the 'goal' is always clear: that which is being worked towards" (ibid.). Furthermore, this "goal" "is reached only when culture 'plays out' its history. Such a culture is never 'immediate' but 'mediated' and separated from the present tense by its own future-orientation" (ibid.).

Repetition, on the other hand, has other, more intricate, aesthetic developments in mind, and "takes place not on a level of musical development or progression, but on the purest tonal and timbral level" (ibid.):

> In black culture, the thing (the ritual, the dance, the beat) is "there for you to pick it up when you come back to it." If there is a goal in such a culture, it is always deferred; it continually "cuts" back to the start, in the musical meaning of "cut" as an abrupt, seemingly unmotivated break (an accidental da capo) with a series already in progress and a willed return to a prior series (ibid.)

As might be understood from this passage, central to black music's penchant for repetition is an inherent coupling with "the prominence of the 'cut'" (ibid.), where this musical device, "overtly insists on the repetitive nature of the music" (1998: 71). The purpose of this "cut," then, might be seen as one of deliberate disruption, somewhat like a gear-shift that ratchets up the intensity of the music upon command.

As a demonstrative of the "cut," Snead finds the music of James Brown exemplarary (1998: 71). The cut, he says, is mobilized through Brown's trademark, punctuating, grunts and groans, similar to that of the "the preacher [who] may cut himself off with phrases such as 'praise God'" (1998: 72). These arbitrary "cuts" in the repetition of Brown's music, most demonstrably in the exhortations to the band to "hit me," or "take me to the bridge," will then drive the music into a new section:

> The format of the Brown "cut" and repetition is similar to that of African drumming after the band has been "cookin'" in a given key and tempo, a cue, either verbal ("Get down" . . .) or musical (a brief series of rapid, percussive drum and horn accents), then directs the music to a new level, where it stays with more "cookin'" or perhaps a solo—until a repetition of cues then "cuts" back to the primary tempo. The essential pattern, then, in the typical Brown sequence is recurrent: "ABA" or "ABCBA" or "ABC (B) A," with each new pattern set off (i.e., introduced and interrupted) by the random, brief hiatus of the "cut" (1998: 71).

The function of the "the cut," then, is perhaps as a conscious invocation of indeterminacy that might produce anticipation through uncertainty. The introduction of the "cut" undermines the certainty of repetition, and, in the process, creates a deliberate sense of anxiety based upon its destabilizing effect. Its irrational nature affirms chance and unpredictability, significant perhaps of the unpredictability of a "God" itself.

Harnessing the uncertainty (and, consequently, the latent anxiety created by this uncertainty) of its arbitrary nature, the "cut" solicits an intensification in the music, where "[t]he ensuing rupture does not cause dissolution of the rhythm; quite to the contrary, it strengthens it, given that it is already incorporated into the format of the rhythm" (ibid.) This complementary role of repetition and "cut" allows for an intricate collective interplay between preacher and congregation as it establishes an indeterminate compositional trajectory, courting, as it does, a productive tension that threatens the stability of the music's continuity. In other words, it renders the composition into an indeterminate state of becoming. This predilection toward the more irrational composition of the gospel form would constitute the most enduring influence on his music, as confirmed here by ex-bandleader and long-time Brown band stalwart, Fred Wesley:

> I think James Brown was tremendously influenced by preachers. When I hear a preacher looking for a note . . . And when he finds that note, then he would work on that one note for a long time. And when he wanted to take it higher he'd say, "take it up a little higher." "A little higher", then "Higher!" And "Higher!" The next thing you know he goes "Higher!" and it becomes a scream (Wesley in Marre [dir.] 2003).

Always willing to point out the church's formidable influence on his formative musical education, Brown would comment, "[m]y music is like a parable . . . When you get happy, you don't quite get enough. An' you just keep doin' it and doin' it and – it's the way people react when they get happy in church. Really I've always gone for that same kind of spiritual concept. Preachers did inspire me: Brother Joe May, Daddy Grace, Rev C L Franklin, Aretha's daddy. And Little Richard, of course" (Brown in Rose 1990: 126). It was likely that Brown bore witness to the style of the preachers during his stint at cleaning out the Trinity Baptist Church, where, following his incarceration, Brown took on the job: "... in order to use their piano ... There was gospel singing and hand-clapping, and the preacher would really get down. I'm sure a lot of my stage show came out of the church" (Brown in Marre [dir.] 2003).

In fact the music of the church is perhaps the most salient indicator of Brown's African past. His adoption of repetition and cut are not only reflective of the gospel aesthetic, but are also demonstrative of membership within a broader aesthetic continuum of Afro-American musical practice. In fact, Brown's act may well be perceived as a secularized dramatization of the more charismatic forms of Christianity as he actively assimilated such gospel staples as *testifying* and *call and response*, all the while maintaining the authority of the "preacher," a position that Brown was rather comfortable with, as witnessed during the autobiographical rap in his anti-drug song, 'Public Enemy #1' (1972), where Brown says with complete sincerity that "... I know when I was a kid they say I was gonna be a preacher ...". Perhaps it is rather unsurprising that, according to Haralambos, Brown's work, "exemplifies many of the features of gospel music that have been incorporated into soul. In 'Shout and Shimmy' he uses falsetto screams and melisma with wild exuberance and does a parody of testifying at the beginning and during the middle of the song" (Haralambos 1974: 101).

It should be noted, however, that in the period of time following the release of 'Please, Please, Please', Brown's forays into straight gospel were very much the exception, with songs such as 'Shout and Shimmy' (1962) or 'Oh Baby Don't You Weep' (1963) only emerging after a period of solid commercial success. Even then, 'Shout and Shimmy' (1962), for example, appeared to have been designed as a knock-off response to the Isley Brothers' sleeper hit, 'Shout' (1959), rather than informing a burgeoning musical aesthetic. Of course, there is the possibility that these records were, in general, significant of a new musical trend hitting the pop record market, the incorporation of gospel fervour into popular song. As Alan Leeds explains in the liner notes to *James Brown: The Singles Volume 2: 1960–1963*, the Isleys' hit, "had been one of the first secular records to unabashedly replicate the spirit of revival meetings: its sparse musical accompaniment was a backdrop for in-your-face tambourines and the brothers' pungent vocals" (Leeds 2007).

While Brown, too, would harness the repetitive incantation that marked the nominally, "primitive" church music (Snead 1998: 71), it would take some time to overtly manifest in his work. Perhaps this was due to its "minority," duly reflected in Syd Nathan's antipathy towards Brown's first commercial composition. Perhaps Brown was aware that relinquishing control of the trajectory or "goal" of the composition goes against Western mores, and, as such, "[a] culture based on the idea of the 'cut' will always suffer in a society whose dominant idea is material progress" (Snead 1998: 69). A preoccupation of continental philosophy for some years, this misunderstanding of repetition has been of particular concern in Deleuze's work, for example. As we are reminded by Richard Middleton, repetition's seemingly simple reiteration of form has ensured centuries of criticism by the European scholar, who would not only unfairly attribute it "primitive" in nature, but use it as evidence of Africa's lack of telos:

> Hegel, Snead points out, defines historical Europe through opposition to its Other – history less Africa. For Hegel, "The Negro represents the Natural Man ... What we actually understand by 'Africa' is that which is without history and resolution, which is still fully caught up in the natural spirit", with all its cyclical rhythms. Inevitably, then, Europe is Master, Africa condemned to be Slave, in Hegel's notorious dialectical figure. But Snead argues that Hegel's description is right, and only his valuation wrong. The awareness and acceptance of the unavoidable repetitiveness of life is a wisdom: "everything that goes around comes around". This enables him to describe the cultivation of repetition in black music, from Africa to James Brown, as a positive, and to welcome its influence on a twentieth-century West gradually releasing repetition from previous repression (Middleton 1996).

While Brown's music has done a lot to alleviate repetition's "repression," its relative value in European culture is still misunderstood. Based on this apparent simplicity of form, and one much in contradistinction to the pre-determined structure or "goal" adhered to in the European compositional tradition, these long-held aesthetic biases have continued to marginalize repetition as cultural artefact.

While repetition in the form of leitmotifs and refrains were similarly fundamental to the European music tradition, it was as discreet content, rather than the totality of compositional structure. The certainty to the compositional logic of the European tradition makes them less "irrational" than styles such as gospel and funk, which might launch into a "cut" at any particular moment.

If one was to make a statement of minority, it would simply be a matter of pushing the possibility of repetition further, which is precisely what Brown would do. Hence we find him locking horns with a resistant record company much concerned over the seeming lack of compositional logic exhibited in a track such as 'Please, Please, Please'.

While it would take another ten years before Brown made repetition a hallmark of his compositional approach via funk, the exploitation of the repetition of the groove had been a feature of gospel long before. Harnessing its power of repetition, funk would embrace gospel's transcendental quality through aleatory incantation rather than preconceived musical trajectory. This is how the groove constitutes the hypnotic state that emancipates from those otherwise inhuman circumstances that its participants had to contend with on a day-to-day basis.

The Irrational Cut

James Brown's use of the "cut" has a corollary with a concept central to Deleuze's discussion of the cinematic time-image, the "irrational cut." Despite its cinematic roots, there are some important features that might elucidate the utility of this concept in examining time in Brown's music, and how it would connect up with dance musics of the future. The importance of the "irrational cut" is that it embraces the power of indeterminacy, whereby,

> the interval suspends the spectator in a state of uncertainty. Every interval becomes what probability physics calls a "bifurcation point" where it is impossible to know or predict in advance which direction change will take. The chronological time of the movement-image fragments into an image of uncertain becoming (Rodowick 1997: 15).

Predicated on a similar notion of an "uncertain becoming," Brown's music implores an immersion in the groove; the jarring cuts throw any preconceived teleological "goal" into disarray, and confront the audience with the uncertainty of time itself. In this sense the use of the irrational "cut" is tantamount to plunging its audience into a creative chaos, or, as Deleuze and Guattari have termed it, a "chaosmos."

The philosophers borrow the concept of the "chaosmos" from the writing of James Joyce (Deleuze and Guattari 1988: 6). The intellectual equivalent of being thrown in the deep-end of a pool without knowing what to do, the chaosmos refers to the artist's capacity to cast themselves into a "consistent chaos" (Deleuze and Guattari 1994: 208) in search of the new. While aggravating and perhaps even painful, it is activity that forces the creative impulse; we learn how to swim in order to navigate the chaosmotic waters that are always potentially fatal (Deleuze and Guattari 1994: 208). The chaosmos is used in relation to the work of art as it effects a productive disruption to the sensibilities of its audience. We might think of the role of the artist as "[opening] up to the Cosmos in order to harness forces in a 'work' (without which the opening onto the Cosmos would only be a reverie incapable of enlarging the limits of the earth)" (Deleuze and Guattari 1988: 337). Art's power is derived from this rediscovery of the infinite as it opens up the possibility of eternal difference. There is a constant movement from "chaos to composition" (Deleuze and Guattari 1994: 203) derived from this discovery of an infinite. Hence it could be understood that a forced assimilation of the chaosmos of co-existent minor temporalities calls forth artistic expression that will structure existential conditions, just as Brown attempted to achieve with the rhythms of funk.

To some, James Brown's music is nothing but banal repetition, often no less than a vamp on a single chord. Yet to sympathetic ears, this repetition evokes the chaosmotic situation of being in the middle of something, the "labyrinth without a thread" (Deleuze 1994: 56). Predicated as it is on repeating a rhythmic pattern with minimal variations, over and over again, the James Brown groove beckons its audience into the unpredictability of its non-linear structure. Any predetermination based on traditional sequential linkages is plunged into this productive chaos, and the audience are forced to rethink preconceived relations of action and reaction. The irrational cut is particularly important to the facilitation of this process, as it precludes a linear evolution of action–reaction, to evoke, instead, one of involution, where time will fold in on itself. This emphasis on the direct experience of difference rather than narrative or compositional convention both confounds and liberates the audience at once. This more direct experience of difference is provided in the gospel style in the following manner: the audience can dispense with an intensive relationship with melodic progression or the "accumulation and growth" of the composition and instead allow themselves to be suspended in time. In this respect we might say that the gospel form successfully dispenses with a fetishizing of the composition and instead implores a direct relation with a "God" as the arbiter of duration in general. If the gospel form looks towards a more transcendental form of time, it is as a method of transgressing the chronological, a means of escape from hegemonic time and space and a substitute for any such emancipation in the actual world.

What the gospel aesthetic would indicate to funk is such a method of temporal transcendence; when the actual present is too intolerable, a minor people might turn to art as a means of conjuring virtual existential territory. This type of collective approach to existential territorializing, for instance, might be demonstrated through the ensemble renditions of the slave songs of the cotton fields. The collective instigation of the musical composition provides temporal and spatial transgression from the madness of the apparent logic that imposes upon their existence.

The ensemble approach to the gospel form of song would at least allow one to transcend singular being and instead become a singing "body without organs" (Deleuze and Guattari 1983: 8), a concept initially proposed by Deleuze and Guattari in *Anti-Oedipus* (1983). The concept, in its most simple sense, might be understood as "the body without an image" (1983: 8), or the body that precedes a social production through its organs. Through song, through rapture, the subject comes closer to being part of a collective, and the forgetting of embodied experience, and becomes otherwise subsumed within a more collective "body."

In his essay, "Becoming-Music: The Rhizomatic Moment of Improvisation," Jeremy Gilbert argues that the becoming at the heart of "recent dance musics and improvised musics" might be perceived as a collective "body without organs." He writes,

> In these moments when the affective morphology of sound takes shapes not easily comprehensible in terms such as "masculine" and "feminine", "order" or "chaos", a becoming-music is enacted which draws a line of flight away from the physical-ideological constraints of the gendered body or fixed musical genres: a body without organs; a smooth, cosmic space (Gilbert 2004a: 126).

This "line of flight away from the physical-ideological constraints of the gendered body or fixed musical genres" constitutes a musically inspired becoming and a forgetting of immanent social constraints. Those scenes of audience members in rapturous exaltation, seemingly overcome by the spirit, or even perhaps, coming out of themselves, are images that we associate with the more charismatic strains of the gospel tradition, an affection that transcends the certainty of logical action or agency. The music thus exploits the interplay of repetition and cut to provide the hypnotic, trance-like state. The audience is given over to concentrating on the joy of the affirmation of the moment rather than concerning themselves with projection. This concentration on the affirmation of the present begins to dominate the predilection for such teleological projection. In its place, then, is an emphasis on the intensity of experience that comes from such repetition. Through a use of distinct periodicities of incantation the preacher can inspire these waves of hysteria teetering on his dynamic directives (or "cuts").

The Splitting of Time

Such concentration on the affirmation of the present means placing one's self in some kind of relation to the incommensurable splitting of time that occurs at each moment. At any given moment we can be overcome by the direct experience of present and yet, at other times, we are equally immersed in the recollection of the past. Each of these relations to actual (present) or virtual (past) segments of time are contained in any instant. As Deleuze says, "there is always a more vast present which absorbs the past and the future. Thus, the relativity of past and future with respect to the present entails a relativity of presents themselves, in relation to each other" (Deleuze 1990a: 162). The common regulation of time, as chronos, is developed around a stabilizing of these temporal bifurcations. This might, for example, include our propensity to delve into the refrains of pure recollection, to maintain our embrace of a direct experience of present. While the church traditions of the African-American as well as that of the European church may both initially involve a form of habit-memory in order to kick off the proceedings, once that is done, the hymns of the white church stick to a navigable path, while those of its black counterpart take flight on an unpredictable course.

We could say that minor cultures are perhaps more inclined to seek other alternate temporal possibilities to a tightly regulated or institutionally sanctioned majoritarian temporality, if only for the reason that this is the time which imposes itself upon their existence. Hence, in some respect the invocation of repetition provides an inadvertent resistance to the majoritarian imposition of the teleological – the maintenance of identity through memorial time and the various syntheses that assist it. As such the "apprehension of a minor temporality" is an attempt at a durational form of expression that serves to express such moments of becoming. Rather than subordinating time as a product of the linear narratives of lived experience, it would instead enable a potential form of apprehension – a bridge between past and present which provokes an active synthesis of memory rather than the passive synthesis of habit. In terms of the latter we could perhaps think of the highly regulated musical protocols of the European church, which attempt to contain becoming, rather than inspire it. By extension we could say that the role of any institution is to regulate, through order, the complex series of rhythms that make up the temporality of our psychic lives.

The gospel form would propose a way to emphasize an alternative conception of time available to composition. This is why I would compare its form to that of the time-image as it produces an image of thought that is non-totalizable and emphasizes a sheer unpredictability alluded to by the irrational cut. Just as I have demonstrated within a musical context, the autonomous interval of the time-image cinema infers that there is no place for thought to maintain identity's dependence on a coherent system of signs. For instance, Deleuze will contend that the movement-image depends on securing the relation between image and thought that will produce identity and, by extension, totality. In contradistinction, the time-image guarantees only the disjunctive and discontinuous, brought about through such irrational divisions and incommensurable relations. This is why we must propose that the time-image is forever combining relations to past and future, subverting both the more tenacious forms of memorial time and habit in a far more complex way than a more linearly structured music.

For the reasons stated above, I believe that Brown's music might be seen to apprehend a minor temporality and an alternate form of time. In terms of musical orientation I think its temporal mode of constitution differentiates it from other contemporary African-American musics, including for example most of jazz that preceded it. While jazz can rely heavily on improvisation, the differences are that jazz tends to resolve in movements, and makes use of signposting refrains to fall back on rather than to overtly modulate a singular refrain. In short, there appears to be a sense of compositional movement even within the most abstract incarnations of the genre. I am not trying to deliberately draw up some dichotomy with jazz here, but rather demonstrate that the forms of music become what they are though their own particular approaches to time, which affects how the body of both performer and audience are realized in time and space. The gospel tradition instead plays on the nuances of singular refrains, and without determined musical signposts it becomes more difficult to find one's direction in the overall trajectory. Hence this form privileges collectivity rather than the singular virtuosity of the soloist of the jazz tradition. This circular method promoted through gospel would prevail, not only in funk, but also in any music that wanted to shift the focus to time rather than movement.

Brown's conception of "the one," in the nascent funk of the mid-1960s, would mobilize the intensity of African-American life, where its "minor" form, derived from gospel, was suitably alien to whites at the time. This musical difference increasingly reflected a preoccupation with time over compositional movement or "goal," which was still the foundation for most forms of popular music styles including the teleological orientation, both of composition and orientation, of the burgeoning soul genre. Whether it was due to his compositional unorthodoxy, pressures from the record company, or a lack of vision on his own part, Brown did not make a record with the repetitive intensity of 'Please, Please, Please' again for quite some time, and in his struggle to follow up its success was unable to dent the charts for another two years (Weinger and White 1991: 19). In this period of uncertainty, Brown seemed to simply follow contemporary musical trends in order to gain commercial acceptance. As Cliff White concedes in the liner notes to *Roots of a Revolution* (1989), "By Brown's own admission, *Chonnie-On-Chon* was a deliberate attempt to rock'n'roll in the style of Little Richard, and *Begging, Begging* an attempt to emulate the slower of Hank Ballad and the Midnighters' two basic styles" (White 1989).

Brown's inability to follow the success of 'Please, Please, Please' found him increasingly threatened with the possibility of being dropped by King; that was, until his career was literally saved by another gospel inspired hit wrested out of the ether, 'Try Me' (1958). The record's plaintive appeal for acceptance was seemingly an outpouring exacerbated by two years in the commercial wilderness. Despite the writer's credit that he gave to himself on the record, whether or not Brown was its actual author is another matter, as Bobby Byrd tells Geoff Brown: "The lyrics James had, he got from this boy down at The

Palms in Hollandale, Florida . . . It was something like the way we got Please, Please (sic) an adaptation from something else. This boy was singing the song around and he gave James the lyric. But it was originally more complicated" (G. Brown 1996: 70). Suffice to say, 'Try Me' gave Brown his first R&B No 1 hit, the best-selling R&B single of the year, and the first of seventeen chart-topping R&B singles over the next two decades.

For the most part, the records of Brown's early period (1956–1962) presented an artist in flux. Without the benefit of retrospect it would be hard to connect him to the sonic innovations he would be responsible for only a few years later on in the decade. In these early years most of his singles were generally orthodox affairs in terms of their composition, although there are some notable exceptions. Among the early Brown catalogue are some moments that indicate, and perhaps even promise, new directions in rhythm. Such titles include the exciting 'I'll Go Crazy' (1960) which boasts a chorus of sage self-assurance even if it bears little resemblance to the rest of the song, "you gotta live, for yourself, yourself and nobody else"; the upbeat rendition of the Five Royales, 'Think' (1960) and the twelve-bar blues based standard first recorded by Jimmy Forrest in 1951, 'Night Train' (1962). But perhaps the most important indication of the coming funk years can be heard via 'I've Got Money' (1962). The latter title is one of the closest things to a nascent funk track, with Clayton Fillyau's New Orleans style drumming given increasing precedence.

Suffice to say, the funk aesthetic was not much in evidence in these formative years. Perhaps it was the ever growing inertia of the civil-rights movement that provided the affective base for Brown's overtures towards the funk aesthetic. Even Brown's relationship to gospel was less than immediately apparent. If Brown would eventually take on the drive and repetition of the gospel experience, then it would be in form rather than narrative content. Gospel's spirituality drove the transcendental optimism of soul, with its appeals to the telos and its mantra that "we shall overcome."

3 The Soul Era

The Roots of Soul

The elevation of soul into a commercially recognized genre has been credited to the attempts of Atlantic Records to market a style that might distinguish the secularized versions of gospel songs recorded by their artist, Ray Charles, from its more churchy competitors. While it is practically impossible to definitively verify the actual genesis of the term "soul," its invention has been claimed both by Charles and also by former president of Atlantic Records, Ahmet Ertegun. It was Ertegun who was sufficiently drawn to this term to name the 1957 album by Ray Charles and Milt Jackson, *Soul Brothers* (Hirshey 1985: 78), based as it was on Charles's new musical direction. As Michael Haralambos explains, "[t]here is general agreement that soul music began in the mid-'50s when Ray Charles, who had formerly sung blues in a style similar to Charles Brown, began to record secular versions of gospel songs" (Haralambos 1974: 100). Ray Charles would transform 'My Jesus Is All World To Me' into the 1954 hit, 'I Got A Woman', and the following year, would give a similar treatment to Clara Ward's old gospel song 'This Little Light Of Mine': "Retitling it 'This Little Girl Of Mine', Ray changed a few words to sing the praises of his girlfriend instead of his maker. The traditionally strict separation of blues and religious music was ended" (Haralambos 1974: 100–101). Even though "[m]any, particularly older people, considered the merging of sacred and secular to be in bad taste" (Haralambos 1974: 100–101), as was recently depicted in the biographical film on Ray Charles, *Ray* (2004), the strict sacred/secular music divide, while quaint in retrospect, was very real at the time.

The ensuing rise of the soul genre courted a re-emphasis on African-American roots music, emerging as it did at a time when the burgeoning civil-rights movement was ready to embrace its aesthetic. For prior to its appearance in the pop music lexicon, "soul" had been used by the jazz community as code for a re-emphasis on apparently "black" aesthetics. As Ertegun himself explains, the term had been commonly circulating among, "black jazz musicians, mainly in New York, in the late fifties and early sixties.

The soul movement in jazz arose as a sort of backlash against the snobbery some musicians felt had invaded and stultified the music and, in effect, made it less black" (Hirshey 1985: 76). Thus, the soul aesthetic would emerge from jazz argot to be absorbed into the general vernacular, a "Black" aesthetic, and an exemplary "minor" mode of expression.

If, in this period of the early 1960s, artists such as Ray Charles and Sam Cooke were the original stars of soul, then by the end of the decade, Brown would surpass them both, no longer just a practitioner, but the very embodiment of the style. Bestowed with monikers such as Soul Brother No. 1 and the Godfather of Soul, Brown would, for the rest of his long career, become synonymous with soul. The reality of the matter, from an aesthetic point of view, was that Brown's music was really only connected to soul in the most superficial way, and as history has borne out, his compositions would increasingly diverge from the discernible styles of his peers. Brown himself would later profess some bemusement about this generic relationship with soul: ". . . don't ask me when they started calling my music soul 'cause I don't remember. It was always that to me" (Brown in Hirshey 1985: 60). The only real connecting factor of the soul styles and Brown's music, as indicated by their work of the mid-1960s, is that both would court the buoyancy of the emergent civil-rights era.

The Civil-Rights Era

The first steps towards an established civil-rights movement came out of the *Brown v. the Board of Education* lawsuit challenging school segregation fought in Topeka, Kansas in 1954. This famous case would produce Afro-America's first official victory over segregation, and, as Ben Sidran contends, "[t]he boost this decision brought to black confidence is inestimable" (Sidran 1995: 126). The inertia that began to build from the case set off a more encompassing struggle, prompting as it did a new wave of anti-segregation cases that would be fought in other states. The decision would, in turn, inspire not only a "new black assertiveness [that] emerged about 1955" but also, "the rise of the 'soul' mystique" (Sidran 1995: 125). The newly inspired sense of assertiveness that came from such victories would positively affect Afro-Americans' image of themselves and the past. Driven by a will to identify, African-Americans would thus begin to more readily embrace their past musical history, including "roots" music, such as gospel, thus setting up the necessary environment from which soul could emerge.

> "Soul" music, then, was one origin of a cultural self-improvement program and, in insisting the Negro had "roots" that were valuable rather than shameful, it was one of the most significant changes to have occurred within black psychology. "Soul" music was important not just as a musical idiom, but also as a black-defined, black-accepted means of actively involving the mass base of Negroes (Sidran 1995: 126).

It is hardly surprising, then, that some of the genre's most famous performers, artists such as the aforementioned Ray Charles and Sam Cooke, as well as Aretha Franklin and Otis Redding later in the decade, would unashamedly assert their relationship to the church through their own particular expressions of the soul aesthetic. For example, Michael Haralambos quotes blues man B. B. King on the differences of soul to blues in terms of audience interaction: "In James [Brown]'s and Aretha [Franklin]'s case they are more like in church, a Holiness church, where everybody's getting the beat, getting the feeling" (Haralambos 1974: 100). The relationship between the soul singers and the gospel experience in terms of inspiring "feeling" is further extrapolated by Haralambos:

> Soul-singers often demand the emotional involvement of their audience in much the same way as gospel singers. James Brown exhorts his audience to "feel good" and "get the feeling" and directs its mood with songs *I Feel Good* and *I Got the Feeling*. Like the lead singer in a gospel group he sings "Hey hey I feel alright" and invites the audience to voice its response (Haralambos 1974: 100).

The sense of collective enunciation voiced by the soul artist was seemingly channelled from the spirit of the civil-rights struggle. Through its musical reiteration, soul inferred a destiny of natural corrective justice that would apparently be delivered through the will of God, a sentiment encapsulated in Sam Cooke's posthumously released classic, 'A Change Is Gonna Come' (1964). Such transcendental narratives would also suggest that maintenance of passivity in the face of one's political goals was a virtue, which, if not rewarded in this world, would apparently be rewarded in the next. Elevating such transcendental "goals" over a more immanent political strategy would not necessarily garner universal favour. Indeed, Malcolm X would famously malign this position and chastise Christian African-Americans for not believing in this world as it was. Malcolm chastised them for dedicating their time to the rousing refrains of 'We Shall Overcome,' when they should "... stop singing and start swinging" (Malcolm X 1992). There was action, of course. The images of the civil-rights demonstration of the early 1960s are well known, and perhaps forever epitomized by the resounding images of the 1963 "March on Washington" where Martin Luther King would deliver his famous, "I Have a Dream" speech to a multi-racial audience.

Soul music wore its heart on its sleeve accordingly. It was referred to by *Billboard* as "music with a philosophy," an up-tempo "black nationalism in pop" (Hirshey 1985: 315), that, "[t]hough clearly not the first aesthetic that mirrored the segregated realities of black life, the soul aesthetic was the cultural component to the most visible black nationalist ideas of the twentieth century" (Neal 2002: 5). It was the first time that this particular section of the population was able to prominently articulate their collective goals and soul's strident narratives would often veer into manifesto, exhibited in songs such as the aforementioned, 'A Change Is Gonna Come' (1964), but also, later on, 'Respect' (1967), or even 'Say It Loud! I'm Black and I'm Proud' (1968) to name but a few more epochal musical moments. Soul's emphasis on narrativizing in its appeal for collectivity would distinguish its lyrical content from the more politically ambiguous themes of the previous rock'n'roll generation. The risqué undercurrent that marks the work of the 1950s wave of rock'n'rollers is instead replaced by the more righteous spirit of the soul period. Unlike the music of this previous wave of African-American popular music artists, soul was very much "grand" narrative-driven, in the sense that the songs deliberately attempted to invoke a universalizing and anthemic quality to aid the struggle for change. Gerri Hirshey makes this observation in reference to an empirical study undertaken by Michael Haralambos in his *Right On: From Blues to Soul in Black America*:

> The "back door man" of the blues had been replaced by the soul man, a lover possessed of both guilt and morality. The "I" of the bluesman had become the "we" in soul music. And having borrowed so much from gospel, soul music was bullish on hope. Activism, while still suicidal in some quarters, had gotten a booster shot of faith with the Civil Rights Act

of 1964. "I Have a Dream," from Martin Luther King, Jr.'s 1963 speech, became the official slogan of radio station WCHB in Detroit. Even WDIA in Memphis adjusted its pitch to "50,000 watts of Soul Power" (Hirshey 1985: 315).

The lyrical shifts that Hirshey remarks on are generally indicative of not only Afro-America's increasing visibility, but also their will to collective identity. As the sixties wore on, and the spirit of the civil-rights agenda grew more apparent, Brown would directly harness this new-found collectivity to the point where his music would appear to enunciate on behalf of the entire Afro-American population. While we have not, in chronological terms, quite reached the stage of Brown's critical mass yet, he continued to make steady progress; throughout the early 1960s Brown would tirelessly tour the "chitlin circuit" (so named after the slang term for "chitterlings/chitlings" which was the intestines of pigs prepared as food), as a means of setting in place the network of goodwill that would crown him Soul Brother No 1 before the decade was out.

Live at the Apollo

The most resounding evidence of this artistic ascent came in the form of breakthrough, *Live at the Apollo* (1963), an album that enjoys a reputation as one of the most celebrated in all of popular music. Long frustrated by the restrictions of the three-minute single, Brown was more than aware that the intricately sequenced repertoire of his live show could only be properly represented in long-playing form. As one hit masterfully segued into another, the intensity of the proceedings building all the while, *Live at the Apollo* allowed audiences to access their own portable version of a complete James Brown show, and its format demanded that the record be heard in full. The subsequent popularity of the album gave rise to an unprecedented situation; radio DJs would not simply select tracks to showcase from the album, but would, instead, just play the entire thing, thus foreshadowing a practice more prevalent of FM broadcasting in the late 1960s.

However, the opposition Brown faced in trying to get the album made is now just as legendary as the content of the record itself. Following the now familiar pattern of rejection established with the release of 'Please, Please, Please', it was no thanks to King boss Syd Nathan who was sure that Brown's proposal for the live album would result in a commercial flop. Bereft of any financial backing from King, the then substantial $5,700 it cost to record the live show would instead have to come from Brown's own pocket (Brown and Tucker 1986: 131). Even after he had fronted the proceeds, Brown still had to fight to get the album distributed. As Peter Doggett wrote in a *Record Collector* article on the album, "King couldn't envisage the record breaking out of the limited market for R&B albums, initially pressing just 5,000 copies" (Doggett 1997: 77). Despite its birthing problems, within a month of its spring 1963 release, *Live at the Apollo* would rise to the No. 2 position on the Pop album charts. That the album would eventually rise so high on this notionally "white" chart was unprecedented for an R&B record (G. Brown 1996: 98–99), and the album's success reflected sales supported by a burgeoning white fan base. Among the teen oriented albums of 1963, *Live at the Apollo* was outsold only by the Beach Boys' *Surfin' U.S.A.* (Doggett 1997: 77).

Rendering the atmosphere of Harlem's Apollo so adroitly, the *Live at the Apollo* album obviously appealed to the many thousands of white kids who could only dream of experiencing a black show first-hand. Replete with the testifying and call and response between performer and audience, the album was perhaps the only conceivable substitute for the real thing that a white listener might have for embracing the "black experience." The enormous success of *Live at the Apollo* is undoubtedly due to its role of intercessor between black and white cultures, not only because the album emerged during a time of actual physical segregation, but also because it gave young white kids another great reason to continue overcoming it.

It has been said that Brown modelled *Live at the Apollo* on Ray Charles's live album, *In Person*, and that the success of Charles's 1962 No. 1 hit "I Can't Stop Loving You" inspired Brown's campaign for "mainstream" acceptance. In pursuit of such "crossover" success, in December 1962 Brown booked sessions with orchestra and chorus. Arranger Sammy Lowe, former trumpeter and composer for Erskine Hawkins's orchestra, had been previously contracted to provide a sophisticated sheen to records by Sam Cooke and the Platters. Out of these sessions Brown would deliver his first "crossover" Top 20 pop single, a radical reworking of the old standard, 'Prisoner of Love' originally released by crooner Russ Columbo in 1931, and perhaps better known from the renditions by Perry Como and Billy Eckstine. For the recording, Brown would utilize a full orchestra, including an eleven-strong string section and nine-voice choir (Leeds 2007).

The 'Prisoner of Love' single was released concurrently with the *Live at the Apollo* album. While, on the one hand, the generic disparity of the releases would indicate Brown's versatility, on the other, it may also have been indicative of some artistic bet-hedging, in the case that Nathan's negative premonition about the live album was indeed correct. Brown's dogged aspirations to position himself as a crossover crooner would prevail to the point of detriment. As he later conceded in his 1986 autobiography, he was sometimes off the mark when it came to judging what his audiences were expecting of him. Booked for a series of dates at the International in Las Vegas in 1970, and convinced that the clientele would be alienated by his regular funk show, Brown weighted his set in favour of standards and show tunes. The booker was incredulous: "If I'd wanted Frank Sinatra . . . I would've hired Frank Sinatra. I was told that everywhere you go you have audiences standing on their seats. Well, I want to see *this* audience standing on *these* seats" (Brown and Tucker 1986: 215). Despite the protestations from the house, Brown took little notice and continued with a set composed of tracks like 'It's Magic' and 'September Song' and consequentially was "dying out there" (Brown and Tucker 1986: 216). Rallying to get the audience on side, Brown would "redo the show on the spot" (Brown and Tucker 1986: 216), and finally give the audience what they actually came to see, a pure undiluted funk experience, and ". . . we *killed* 'em. Dead" (Brown and Tucker 1986: 216).

Given the runaway success of *Live at the Apollo*, one might expect that Brown's artistic vision was crystal clear, yet there is evidence that this was not quite the case. That Brown was somewhat unsure of what direction to take at this juncture is evident in some of the artistic choices made in the aftermath of that watershed album. In 1963, Brown attempted to emulate the successes of the previous year by recording more standards, and then overdubbing them with fake audience applause. Such was the case with the overdubbed collection of old R&B standards to be found on the album *Showtime* (1964), which Brown then followed with, even more, on the *Out of Sight* album. Apparently lacking direction, Brown was let off the hook, "when the title track became a break-out dance hit of 1964" (White 2000).

Out of Sight was remarkable for its commercial success, but even more remarkable for its status as one of the first key indications of where Brown's music would be heading in the future. While both he and the record company should have been basking in its success, the ongoing artistic disagreements at King gave Brown reason to negotiate a new deal with rival label, Mercury.

Given that he was still legally contracted to make records for King, most of the rest of that year was taken up with legal ranglings, and, in the end, Brown continued recording at Mercury, under the Smash imprint, as an instrumentalist only. All vocal productions would remain the property of King forthwith, although under slightly more favourable financial circumstances.

Between the two labels, Brown maintained a prodigious output throughout the mid-1960s. Dance oriented albums, jazzy instrumentals, ballads, gospel tracks, Brown's albums continued to clutch at a grab bag of styles. This ability to diversify would only help Brown to maintain his popularity when so many of the other soul artists "went down with the ship" in the late 1960s. The alterity contained within Brown's idiosyncratic approach to the music of the soul period would elicit a collection of literal forces that would serve music into the future. For, despite his music's generic attribution, Brown's style would retreat from the more narrative-based form found in most soul music of the time, to instead embark on a style that would apprehend the broader existential *forces* that harnessed the full potential of time in musical form. The difference between Brown's approach, and that of the broader soul movement, might be summed up as the living difference between 'A Change is Gonna Come' and 'Papa's Got a Brand New Bag', two archetypal soul songs that were released within a year of each other, in 1965, and both at the very apex of the soul movement.

Soul as Movement-image

The spirit embodied in the slogan, 'A Change is Gonna Come', points to the overwhelming optimism that accompanied the soul aesthetic up until at least the mid-1960s. The philosophical position of the movement was one driven by a teleological notion of Truth propelling a sense of social justice that would transpire via a series of linear, common sense, and unified chronological events. This belief in a telos and of action–reaction, leading to a "natural" social progression, might be constitutive of soul's "movement-image." Similar to the context that Deleuze attributes to his cinematic example, soul follows a mode of thought that "intuitively" organizes what is presumed to be the "organic" logic of time, which derives the temporal from an accumulation of actions (movements). This is the form of time that Deleuze would refer to as "organic" because it reiterates a "common sense" notion of meaningful, teleological, linear flow. It is a time that is aligned to a conception of actions (movements) that transpire from the natural orientation of the "sensory-motor-schema," or a proclivity towards action–reaction which we attribute as "common sense." As D. N. Rodowick explains:

> The indirect image of time restricts itself to the sensorimotor schema. Movements are represented as actions prolonging themselves in space as reactions, thus generating chains of narrative cause and effect in the form of linear succession. Ultimately, the sensorimotor schema implies a world apprehensible in an image of Truth as totality and identity. The movements of thought are exhausted in the dialectical image of an ever-expanding spiral and in the belief of a world mastered by action (Rodowick 1997: 84–85).

What we might understand from this is that time is only made visible secondarily, as its primary function is the accumulation of movements within the sensory-motor-schema. It is this more conventional notion of time that, in Deleuze's cinematic analysis, drove early cinema up to the post-war period. It is also this conventional understanding of time that underpinned the existential perspective of the soul movement: a perspective that narrativized time and perhaps artificially connected it to a unified and actionable will-to-truth. In this sense the soul movement was entirely modernist in that it was driven by an idea of the world geared to a teleologically driven set of convictions. This is perhaps why Mark Anthony Neal ascribes to the soul aesthetic, "the most vivid and popular expression of an African-American modernity" (Neal 2002: 3). Imbuing soul with a modernist trajectory is not a point of criticism nor a denigration of the amount of thought, work and suffering that went into these appeals for a new type of existence. The point of concern is how soul would deliver such promise to those who either could not, or did not, adhere to its schema.

Hence the real power of political change, which tends to elude macro-politics, might be more readily achieved through the micropolitics of desire and *what a body could do*. These are glimpses that might be found in "the frenzy of Aretha Franklin's voice or the syncopated choreography present in any James Brown performance" (Neal 2002: 4). A more productive political approach might be to concentrate on the bodily reactions breaking out of historical events. The affects that these produce effect as real a transformation of the social as teleological narrative unity, if not more so. While at the time, such glimpses were dramatic, even they demonstrated the vast virtual potential of a body. Yet, while I will argue that these gestures were indicative of a new political visibility, this visibility had its price. The power of a body given such new-found social freedoms meant that it was often working against the narratives that mobilized it in the first place. This is why we shall see that in the aftermath of soul's faith in the universal notions of movement the emphasis will shift instead to the ethical power of individual bodily movement. Perhaps the ultimate lesson of music is that there is nothing to believe in but the ethics behind specific interactions with other bodies.

The *T.A.M.I. Show*

If anyone had within them the capacity to renegotiate what a body could do, then such a capacity might be witnessed in James Brown's intensive stage show, which was at its peak in the mid-1960s. Given the fact that his stagecraft is considered extraordinary even decades later, one wonders just what the audiences of the time might have made of it, especially as he began his campaign for crossover appeal. An important event in helping his crossover was via his much lauded performance on the 1964 *T.A.M.I. Show*. Taped in front of a live, and more importantly for the time, a multi-racial audience, the *T.A.M.I. Show* broadcast (the acronym *T.A.M.I.* has alternately been used in reference to the titles Teenage Awards Music International and Teen Age Music International) has perhaps taken on more historical significance as time has gone by, and as Marc Eliot comments in his book on Brown, the *T.A.M.I.* performance is "universally regarded as the most astonishing performance in the entire history of rock and roll" (Eliot 2005: 29).

This now-legendary concert event alternated between both black and white popular music's biggest stars, where Brown's performance took place alongside acts as diverse as the Beach Boys, Ray Charles, Smokey Robinson and the Miracles, Chuck Berry, the Supremes and the Rolling Stones. As Peter Guralnick offers in his book, *Feel Like Going Home*, the broadcast offered White America's first contact with Brown's extraordinary stage show, even if it was the appearance of the Rolling Stones that provided a lure, and which initiated this contact with Brown:

> Of all their contributions to my own education, though, I would say that the one for which I was most grateful was the presence of James Brown in The Stones-headlined *T.A.M.I.*

Show film. James Brown, of course, we had heard of, we knew his music a little, and his reputation as an entertainer preceded him. Nothing that we heard could have prepared us for what we saw even in the grainy, far-away quality of the film. The dynamism, the tireless energy and unflagging zeal, the apocalyptic drama of his performance were all unprecedented in our experience, and when we emerged from the theatre we had the idea that we could skate one-legged down Washington Street, defying gravity and astonishing passers-by. The Stones after that performance had been nothing more than an anti-climax, and we watched in silent approval as the blacks trooped out one by one, leaving the field to the latecomers (Guralnick 1971: 28–30).

Retrospective accounts given by members of both the Rolling Stones and Brown's band have recounted that Brown's extraordinary performance at T.A.M.I. was driven by retribution, angered as he was by the fact that he was relegated from top-billing by a then comparatively unknown Rolling Stones. Brown was rumoured to "make the Rolling Stones wish they'd never come to America" (Wyman 1990: 271) and, to make sure of this, he would add an even more ferocious intensity to what was already an unprecedented spectacle. The four songs 'Out of Sight', 'Please, Please, Please', 'Prisoner of Love' and 'Night Train', performed by Brown and the Famous Flames, were captured on film for posterity. Brown's performance of 'Night Train', in particular, is considered one of the most enticing spectacles in the history of popular music. It has been said that Elvis Presley used to watch it nightly, and that Michael Jackson built a career on it (Hirshey 1985: xii). Brown and his bands had been arduously making the rounds of the chitlin circuit for a decade, and they were operating at another level entirely. Thus Brown's bitterness over the white musicians' attempts at recolonizing African-American musical territory was entirely justifiable. The result was extraordinary. As Marc Eliot has commented, the show helped to usher in Brown's crossover to the white mainstream through a performance, "in which he changed forever the face and course of popular music, and the teen culture that looked to it for its anthemic identity" (Eliot 2005: 29). Many of the white teens watching became instant converts. Accounts of the performance are given pride of place by the white authors of texts on soul, such as Gerri Hirshey (1985: xii), Peter Guralnick (1971: 28–30), Marc Eliot (2005: 29) and others as a decisive and life-changing moment that would inspire their own personal journeys into soul music fanaticism.

Despite Brown's bravado, both sides were reportedly as nervous as the other; Bobby Byrd later commenting that the Famous Flames were just as scared of the Rolling Stones as the Stones were of them. The Flames didn't want to be put up against the Stones, but rather placed between the Motown acts that they thought they could beat (G. Brown 1996: 114). Of course they needn't have worried, as Brown's performance on the *T.A.M.I. Show* raised the popular music performance to an unprecedented level of intensity. The effect was almost immediate. Having to directly follow Brown on the *T.A.M.I. Show*, Mick Jagger would step up his level of animation quite discernibly in response (G. Brown 1996: 114). To put Brown's performance in context, one has to merely compare its intensity with the quaint respectability of the other acts on the bill. While Smokey Robinson and the Miracles may have also included some extravagant choreography, they were not screaming and crying and running across the stage on one leg.

Brown's audaciously uncompromising performance was even more radical given the fact that the whole concept of desegregated shows and audiences was only fully legalized a few months previous when President Lyndon Johnson signed the Civil Rights Act of 1964 into law. The act officially outlawed the segregation of public places such as libraries, swimming pools, theatres, restaurants, and hotels. Within this climate, package-shows such as T.A.M.I. were no less than pioneering social experiments. These shows would be instrumental in revealing new sections of previously marginal American cultures.

Countering the British Invasion

In fact, a more realistic scenario is that, for most black popular music artists, one marginal situation was simply replaced by another. As white musicians were able to approximate covers of their R&B idols, their audience were necessarily alleviated of the complications of broader interracial assimilation. Indeed the white appropriation of the black pop market conspired to destroy the momentum of black musicians gaining a foothold in a broader section of the pop market. As Ben E. King says in the "Be My Baby" episode of the BBC documentary series, *Dancing in the Street* (1996):

> There was a bit of jealousy because we were cut off at a time when we just getting ready to be stronger ourselves [Black pop performers] . . . All signs were there that the music being created right here at home was going to be tremendously big and then all of a sudden these kids came along (the Beatles) and stopped all that . . . and it was a strong pill to swallow . . . and I think the only one to survive that thing was someone like James Brown who was so far to the left of what they were doing that it didn't affect him. So James covered all of what was going on and what Blacks felt they needed musically to survive the Beatles thing.

Among these "British Invasion" artists that King refers, Brown's music remained somewhat of an anomaly, and certainly not covered as readily as the music of other more orthodox soul artists had been. The covers of the bulk of the white musicians such as the aforementioned Rolling Stones gravitated toward the more orthodox types of soul songs of performers such as Solomon Burke and Marvin Gaye. The Rolling Stones, for example, recorded Burke's 'Everybody Needs Somebody to Love', 'That's How Strong My Love Is' and 'Cry to Me' found on the (UK versions) of *The Rolling Stones No. 2* and *Out of Our Heads* (both 1965) LPs and Gaye's 'Can I Get a Witness?' and 'Hitch Hike' on the (UK versions) of *The Rolling Stones* (1964) and *Out of Our Heads* (1965) LPs.

Brown's immunity to these commercial threats from the "British Invasion" were thwarted due to his rather unique musical situation; his intricate big band sound insured him somewhat against appropriation by the smaller British beat combos. The threat of the British groups, just like the appearance of the Stones at *T.A.M.I.*, perhaps led Brown to more radical feats of musical creativity, more "minor," and perhaps even less accessible to covers by white groups. Brown would instead retain a more underground, cult status among niche groups such as the Mods, whose propensity was to embrace the more marginal of the soul artists. So when Brown was covered, it was by Mod favourites The Who, perhaps due to the fact that lead singer Roger Daltrey was one of the few that possessed the vocal range necessary to cover the song in the first place (G. Brown 1996: 136). Despite The Who's valiant attempts to make inroads into the Brown catalogue, music scholar Craig Werner duly describes these attempts as, "[t]he low point of obsession with black American music" (Werner 2000: 82).

Appropriation or Becoming?

The reservations about the way black music was "covered" have prompted much commentary. In particular, those who reduce the situation to mere "appropriation" do not fully account for the dynamism and complexity of such a cultural encounter. A classic example of the type of criticism that lambasts the "dilution at the hands of white appropriation" is described here in Dave Headlam's "Appropriations of Blues and Gospel in Popular Music" (2002) (Headlam 2002: 180). Headlam writes that the covers of black blues and gospel music by white artists strip the music of its authenticity and provide their respective audiences instead with a "watered-down form," "with their original meanings lost" (Headlam 2002: 161). Headlam thinks such appropriation is symptomatic of the white person's desire for the black "grain of the voice," a concept famously coined by Roland Barthes (Headlam 2002: 161). Barthes's "grain" is a "texture in the sound and the associated expression is a human element interpreted as a physical and emotional effort that resonates with listeners, as they relate the emotions to their own lives" (Headlam 2002: 161). For Headlam, the white emulation of the black "grain of the voice" is depthless, a testament to style over substance, as "the original performers and creators of the expression and its social meanings tend to be left behind in such cultural transactions" (Headlam 2002: 161).

The problem with this argument, however, is that it depends on maintaining a distinction between an authentic model, and copies of that model regarded as somehow "lesser" to the original. While it is tempting to discuss how "white appropriation" may have diluted the "authenticity" of black music, I believe that it is just as fruitful to put such critique of "appropriation" aside to consider to the extent that whites were also becoming in these cultural encounters. The becoming that transpires through such cultural engagement is not merely the embracing of a nominal identity or attempting to pass one's self off *as something*. It is at this moment when becoming is rendered self-conscious, a futile qualification of an untenable claim of authenticity, rather than an engagement of productive difference with the culture at hand. Furthermore, under no circumstances should the resultant series of becomings be merely limited to the idea of a performer projecting a new appropriated identity, for the reality is anything but. Perhaps the most enticing aspect of playing "black" music was not to appropriate the music, or even the performer's identity so much as to attempt to interact with the experience of the specific time-space of its performer. The white musicians' attempts to play this music gave them a space to play out their own alterity, or to develop their own difference (rather than, say, adopt blackness per se) in a relatively (for then) socially acceptable way. In short, the interactions of white musician and black music can still ultimately be considered as a becoming, even though such becoming might not necessarily produce an attendant economic equality. I am well aware that, at least in economic terms, such encounters inordinately benefit the white performer "covering" the song, at the expense of the black "original." I am aware, too, that though becoming-black, the temporary dissolution of a categorical "whiteness," will never correspond into an equivalent "blackness," but will continually involve a departure from majoritarian "whiteness." As Dyer comments, these cultural biases towards white are still part of popular construction of white, as majoritarian, as neutral territory: "The wide application of white as symbol, in non-racially specific contexts, makes it appear neutral: white as good is a universal abstraction, it just happens that it coincides with people whose skin is deemed white" (Dyer 1997: 70).

The becoming of the white artist in "covering" black music should however be differentiated from rather more disconcerting precedents. Such "covers" are quite distinct from the kind of ill-conceived emulation found in, for example, the "cooning" of minstrelsy, where the latter might otherwise demonstrate the crass results of a more generalized concept of representation. In this type of example, the problem is one of starting with an idea of representation rather than to look first at the affective connection (as found, for example, in the song of the performer), as a vehicle that might enable an alterity to be divulged through its repetition.

This does of course rely on whether this is imitation, which is the opposite of becoming. For imitation is the opposite of becoming, a point explained here by Deleuze and Guattari:

> Suppose a painter "represents" a bird; this is in fact a becoming-bird that can occur only to the extent that the bird itself is in the process of becoming something else, a pure line and pure color. Thus imitation self-destructs, since the imitator unknowingly enters into a becoming that conjugates with the unknowing becoming of that which he or she imitates ... Becoming is never imitating (Deleuze and Guattari 1988: 304–305).

The problem is that "representation as identity" operates via similitude and tends towards a generalization that avoids specificity. This is of course precisely the sort of essentialist trap that Deleuze warns of in *Difference and Repetition*, where he argues for the heterogeneous, specific and always unfinished nature of becoming rather than the generalized attributes made between model and copy (Deleuze 1994: 126–28). For becoming is the process of difference in effect, a repetition of difference that cannot be arrived at through the "uncovered or bare repetition" of imitation (Deleuze 1994: 17–18). This uncovered repetition refers to the type of mechanical repetition of the Same that underscores the similitude adhered to through ceremony or via the stereotype. A "covered" repetition, on the other hand, is a repetition which has difference hidden within itself. As Deleuze writes, "The mask, the costume, the covered is everywhere the truth of the uncovered. The mask is the true subject of repetition. Because repetition differs in kind from representation, the repeated cannot be represented: rather, it must always be signified, masked by what signifies it, itself masking what it signifies" (Deleuze 1994: 18).

It would be to the detriment to the vast and real becomings that occurred in these musical interactions to suggest that it is all imitation, even if that may have been the case in certain repetitions of the form. Espousing appropriation is to accept the banal estrangement of model and copy, and perhaps undermines the more fruitful interactions that have occurred between once estranged bodies, and furthermore, limits the body undergoing these transformations to the most general form of representation.

What Can a Body Do?

For the body should not be simply thought of as a lesser material extension of a (greater) subject, nor of fixed biological form, but should be considered on the basis of its capacities to affect new relations in the world. To concentrate on the micropolitical dimension of desire is to imagine a body as the basis of a belief in the specific, complex and fluid world as it is, rather than confined in the body to the product of an adherence to ideology or dogma. In fact, Deleuze remarks, after Spinoza, that a belief in the world is a belief in the body itself (Deleuze 1989: 172):

> What is certain is that believing is no longer believing in another world, or in a transformed world. It is only, it is

simply, believing in the body. It is giving discourse to the body, and, for this purpose, reaching the body before discourses, before words, before things are named . . . (Deleuze 1989: 172–73).

An actual belief in the world is not to be found through *our knowledge* of the world but only through an experimentation of the body (including of course the brain) that might connect to *the* world. We need to remain open to the possibility that man and the world will be once again connected (Deleuze 1989: 172). The importance of the "minor" artist or the "minor" language is to facilitate such connections to the world as it actually *is*, rather than to the world's *representation* by dominant thought. As Rajchman writes, " 'Minor languages' like Black English pose this problem – one must devise ways of being at home not in a territory but in this Earth, which, far from rooting them in a place, an identity, a memory, releases them from such borders . . ." (Rajchman 2000: 95).

The most effective catalyst for release is art, to remind us of the affective possibilities of the body: "Not that the body thinks, but, obstinate and stubborn, it forces us to think, and forces us to think what is concealed from thought, life" (Deleuze 1989: 189). As I will discuss in the next chapter the creative power of life emerges as a result of the naïve figure asking, "why can't I do this?" To ask one's self such a question is the first step to connection rather than limitation, and, as I have briefly outlined above, orienting a body to an embrace of connection rather than judgemental difference is one of Deleuze's (and Guattari's) most fundamental concerns:

> We know nothing about a body until we know what it can do, in other words, what its affects are, how they can or cannot enter into composition with other affects, with the affects of another body, either to destroy that body or to be destroyed by it, either to exchange actions or passions with it or to join with it in composing a more powerful body (Deleuze and Guattari 1988: 257).

To provide for the affective connections that might ameliorate "becomings rather than stories" is the ethical challenge of the *Cinema* books.

If the search for truth produces a body it does so in an unexpected way. For instance, we might find ourselves searching for the truth about a subject (of a body) and the process will, in turn, require our assimilation of images of that subject (and body) to produce the desired result. However, the paradox that Deleuze brings up is that the more images we seek in relation to the "truth" about something, the more potential for difference actually emerges. The quest for a "truthful" image of an authenticity will only bring difference to the fore.

Overcoming the Limits of Representation

In fact if anyone was celebrated for their "authenticity," it was the mid-1960s James Brown. Yet, despite the wealth of commentary on Brown's "blackness," and his apparently uncompromising negation of the "inauthentic" Negro or coloured person, Brown too was struggling to "become black." In his own specific way, Brown was able to redefine what it meant to be "black" in the world, and, furthermore, redraw the limits once enforced upon the "black" body.

While we can rightly celebrate Brown's capacity to articulate the concept of being "black," just as he would in 'Say It Loud! I'm Black and I'm Proud' (1968), we can also witness how Brown himself would articulate this minor position subsumed as he was within the limits of representation that he himself suffered. Brown himself struggled to become black, and his creativity was fuelled by the fact that he was actually marginal within his own culture. For example, Brown's childhood friend and revue member, Leon Austin, describes Brown as being "dark skinned," a real impediment for an African-American trying to crossover. Describing Brown's appearance on the *Ed Sullivan Show*, Hirshey writes

> James Brown cut loose with a swaggering pride few men of color dared express in mixed company. Even among blacks, it ruptured the stratification of "high complexion" versus low. "A darker person would probably be named as ugly," Leon explains. And James Brown is dark. "So," says Leon, "he made the ugly man *somebody*" (Austin in Hirshey 1985: 285).

Austin's distinction somehow inferred that this made Brown's accomplishments all the more empowering for the many previously invisible African-Americans forced to endure a similar marginalization at the time (ibid.).

Black and Proud

Given this environment of precarious aesthetic qualification, a more positive, self-determined racial descriptor was obviously required. The first signs of a discursive shift from "Negro" to "black" emerged as an effect of 1960s activism, including the formation of the *Black Panther* movement in 1966 (Vincent 1996: 51). In her 1967 publication "Revisiting 'Black Power', Race and Class," Marxist scholar, Raya Dunayevskaya, cites the importance of Stokely Carmichael (Kwame Ture) who as chairman of the SNCC (Student Non-Violent Coordinating Committee) from May 1966 to June 1967, would popularize the slogan "Black Power" (Dunayevskaya 1967). Yet the term only truly reached critical mass through Brown's 'Say It Loud! I'm Black and I'm Proud', which was a particularly important development in displacing the outmoded "Negro" (Vincent 1996: 55).

Of course Brown too would have to face the terms of his representation and perhaps become minor, become *black*, in response. In fact it was Brown's own minority within a minor culture, as an "uneducated," "dark-skinned" (Austin in Hirshey 1985: 285) man that perhaps further led him to take a marginal position and give it not only a new sense of presence, but with that presence the belief of being able to connect with the world. This is perhaps why so many African-Americans loved him, because he was a political figure in a way that was not even known, or understood, by the white majority –this majority of course in the Deleuze-Guattarian sense, of the dominant culture rather than the numerical majority. In contrast to a performer such as Little Richard, James Brown would appeal to the minor. For instance, Richard speaks here of Brown's distinct appeal to Black America: "James Brown was different from me. He was big to the black market. When he came to town, you would get ten thousand blacks. When I came to town, you would get ten thousand whites, and about ten blacks" (Richard in White 1985: 153).

It would probably be fair to attribute some of Richard's lack of sustained success (if viewed in relation to Brown's) within the general African-American community to a discomfort with Richard's overt homosexuality. (Richard's breakthrough single 'Tutti Frutti' (1956) was a thinly disguised allusion to his sexuality, where the original lyrics concerning a gay male with a good behind, "Tutti Frutti, good booty / If it don't fit don't force it / You can grease it, make it easy . . ." (Richard in White 1985: 55) were changed to the more ambiguous "tutti frutti . . . aw rooty" by co-writer Dorothy La Bostrie (Richard in White 1985: 50–51). As black culture *in general* was strange enough to whites, most of his original teenage audience probably had little idea about his sexuality and embraced him for his more general reflection of otherness. The layers of pancake make-up he has worn through his career (White 1985: 144) may also have been read as an appeal to "whiteness" and a position of stark contrast to Brown's apparent "ugliness," which his friend Leon Austin attributed as Brown's "common man" appeal within the African-American community (Austin in Hirshey 1985: 285). For Brown maintained a sense of aspiration that betrayed the social limitations of the "darker skinned black," and it is perhaps for this reason that Brown, in the tradition of the Deleuze-Guattarian minor author, would inspire a greater appeal to collectivity.

The notion of "dark skinned" here refers to the deep-seated skin-tone hierarchy, a rather arcane process of differentiation used by African-Americans that has its roots in assimilation with the majoritarian culture. Brown had to shake off a legacy where the white audience would expect their "Negroes" to be as Caucasian looking as possible, and the mainstream success of artists such as Lena Horne, Johnny Mathis or Nat "King" Cole was predicated on their ability to pass. "Blackness" as an identity was a goal still yet to be mobilized into mainstream recognition in any overt way. In fact, a skin colour hierarchy persists to this day, an unfortunate albeit tenacious vestige of colonialism in general. It has been the subject of frequent discussion, including the following journal articles, "Shades of Brown: The Law of Skin Color" (Jones 2000) and "Hey Girl, Am I More Than My Hair?: African American Women and their Struggles with Beauty, Body Image, and Hair" (Patton 2006). The latter subject was recently turned into a feature film, by Chris Rock, entitled *Good Hair* (2009). In fact one of the very interesting points of that film was that Brown acolyte, adopted son, and social activist, Rev Al Sharpton, explains to Rock that it was Brown who introduced him to the world of the "process" (chemical straightening), a hair crime that Brown could not stop himself committing. If Brown would re-embrace the Afro, in his late 60s–early 70s Black and Proud period, it was a gesture to the black community rather than a conviction. Brown's personal aesthetic, tainted as it was by his contact with a society that privileged white aesthetics, was so deeply indoctrinated that wearing a "process" was simply natural to him. There is, of course, a rather strange set of tensions at work here. Despite Brown's equation with "blackness," Brown was also trying to "become-black." For rather than being absolute, "blackness" (and in particular a diasporic blackness) is always dynamic, subjected as it is to its own hierarchies and stratification.

Brown publicly played out the inherent tensions and contradictions of such blackness, and furthermore he dared to "feel good," regardless of the skin he was in. The melancholic laments of the blues idiom were being replaced with exuberant paeans to life in general. This was political, then, in the sense that such a blatant espousal of "feeling good" not only directly challenged the majoritarian persuasion toward the maintenance of the Protestant work ethic, but also because it claimed bodily pleasure – indeed particular bodily pleasures – as a right. On the most banal level of pure representation, Brown's dynamic physicality on-stage was a visible signal of a more audacious presence of non-white people, doing apparently non-white things. The dynamism of James Brown's stage show was ready to make a mockery of (white imposed) Puritanical mores. Indeed, if one is to express an assemblage that would directly challenge such mores, why not call it funk?

Brown's music made positive gestures towards the future through lyrical narrative, but its main power was activating the presence of bodily potential. The rendering visible of the presence of the body, of what were previously invisible bodies and untapped bodily forces, becomes a sort of directly expressed "manifesto" of the possible. Such a rendering visible of these forces helps us to understand why Deleuze says that a belief in the world is a belief in the body. The way Brown screamed on mainstream TV, together with his frenetic dancing style, challenged the dominance of a more discreet Puritan ethic. In the words of Peter "Blackie" Black, a member of Australian punk rockers The Hard-Ons, "[h]ow hardcore is this man, that during a racist era he would strut across the stage dripping in sweat, singing 'I feel like a sex machine'?" (Black 2001: 24).

While Sidran had previously lamented soul's lack of political import, accusing it of "being nothing but party music," we can see from Blackie's comments that just being a black man having a good time on stage was actually a political statement in and of itself. Sidran seems to have recognized Brown's uniqueness in this environment, as the Godfather escapes his damning assessment of the soul genre:

> It should be stressed that James Brown's screams and the two drummers he employed to generate an enormous rhythmic dynamism were more revolutionary than were his somewhat controversial lyrics, which included "I'm Black and I'm Proud" and "Don't want nobody to give me nothing, open the door, I'll get it myself," especially because they were not recognised as being revolutionary. The techniques of the oral culture thus met with little opposition and altered the perception, and so the behaviour, of young Americans in the privacy of their own homes (Sidran 1995: 147).

Brown was of course becoming increasingly visible to the mainstream, enjoying exposure on the previously off-limits bastions of family entertainment such as the *Ed Sullivan Show* on which he appeared in 1966. As the living testament to some of the gains being made by the civil-rights movement, Brown was able to speak to a broad cross-section of mainstream Afro-America in a language that was discernibly theirs. His uncompromising style only reinforced his minority; there were few other mainstream entertainers that so brazenly punctuated their songs with those inimitable screams, grunts and squeals for which Brown would become synonymous. These utterances articulate an emergent minor presence far better than the enunciation of the easily framed and common sense "see-able and the say-able" ever could.

If Amiri Baraka (LeRoi Jones) had once hailed the "wilfully harsh, anti-assimilationist sound of bebop" (Jones 1963: 181–82) as the epitome of Black musical resistance, by the time of his 1967 book *Black Music*, he would revise this assessment in favour of what Brown was doing at the time:

> James Brown's screams . . . are more "radical" than most jazz musicians sound . . . Certainly his sound is "further out" than Ornette's. And that sound has been a part of Black music, even out in them backwoods churches since the year one. It is just that on the white man's instrument it is "new." So, again, it is just life need and interpretation (Jones 1967: 210).

Seen perhaps from another angle, Brown asserted political power precisely because people didn't even recognize such uses of the body as political. One can juxtapose Brown's performances with performances of other soul stars like Marvin Gaye or Smokey Robinson to see how radical was Brown's vocal technique. Much removed from the dulcet tones of his peers, Brown's style was something between singing and "screaming," and seemed to reflect all of the horror experienced by African-Americans across time within a singular utterance. Brown's trailblazing, gospel infused frenzy of emotion set the stage for the similarly frenetic vocals of an Otis Redding or an Aretha Franklin that followed later in the decade.

Brown further galvanized the minor community via idiom and street slang, a language that was in a continual process of becoming-minor and, by nature, eschewed an assimilation of the majority. A minor language must articulate the becoming of a future, and Brown's expression of a minor temporality, musically, linguistically and otherwise, necessarily intervened and provided a belief in the world when the narratives of soul fell apart. In view of the decline of soul's appeal to majoritarian assimilation, the more minority oriented sections of the African-American population were less affected as they had always realized that were not part of that society's narrative anyway.

Brown's focus on the groove is indicative of this investment in a micropolitics of minority becoming, rather than the more macro-political concerns of hegemonically inspired narrativizing. It provides a set of conditions allowing the virtual potential of bodies to engender new connections and affects. Any limit to the body's ability to become is always as much a product of social conditions as any inherent physical limitation. Yet becoming does not wait for either of these to "catch up" with its drive forward. Awareness of this fact marks the critical difference between soul saying "in time" and Brown saying "now," or the fundamental difference in outlook between "a change is gonna come" and Papa having "his brand new bag" and audaciously expressing it.

For no matter how well intentioned the goals of the soul aesthetic and the accompanying civil-rights movement, they were ultimately directed to addressing change that *might* occur at some unspecified time in the future. For while it enjoyed a window of opportunity lasting roughly a decade, the soul movement would ultimately suffer from a problem that besets most "movements": the philosophical dependence on a belief in a kind of teleological time that is disconnected from the present. However, rather than placing one's faith in time as a revelatory process, a minor people should not define their future through a majoritarian interpretation of time and space, but instead show up the deficiencies of majoritarian determination. Brown's artistic experimentations took that shift from the telos to new bag, from narrative to non-linear approach to time.

In this respect, the story of Brown's funk becomes a story about what a body could do – the re-institution of a belief in the potential of the world – as an aesthetic that embraced the *now*. His music conveyed the relationship between a belief in the world and a belief in the body that might hopefully move beyond an imposed "common sense" image of thought. Hence the reason we turn to music and the performing artist is because both push the boundaries of what a body can do in the world; they instil within us a belief in the capacities of bodies to overcome the histories that define their actions. This is where the world of present, real potential becomes that of a "people to come" – in motion, in becoming, this can only begin with new kinds of bodies.

4 The Foundations of Funk

The invention of funk has long been considered solely Brown's to claim. To quote hip-hop pioneer, Fab 5 Freddy from his book, *Fresh, Fly, Flavor* (1992), "'funky' is used for everything to do with music, fashion, culture or ideas that comes from a black background, and in a special sense for any cultural achievement inspired by the Godfather of soul James Brown" (Poschardt 1998: 417). Yet the term funk had actually been kicking around since at least the turn of the twentieth century, initially "brought to musical prominence in the title of a jazz tune called 'Funky Butt' by a New Orleans jazz cornetist, Buddy Bolden, around the 1900s" (Keyes 2002: 41). Celebrated in song via Jelly Roll Morton's 'I Thought I Heard Buddy Bolden Say' (1939), it was the latter title that integrated the term funk more fully into jazz lexicon. Hard bop pianist, Horace Silver, would subsequently make use of the term in the 1950s "to define the return to the evocative feeling and expressiveness of traditional blues" as captured in his 'Opus de Funk' (1953) (ibid.).

In the context of jazz, a funky style was synonymous with an approach imbued with authenticity and "to call a composition, a passage, or a player funky was not only to offer praise in general, but a means of lauding the object of praise for its specifically black qualities" (Kofsky 1970: 44). Despite its usage among jazz musicians, funk was vernacular for "the smell of sex" (Rose 1990: 46–47) and not a term to be used in polite company. As Maceo Parker, the young saxophonist who helped Brown bring his funk blueprint to fruition, recalls, "I do remember havin' to get that term 'funk' OK'ed by my parents, and some of my peers havin' to get it OK'ed by *their* parents . . . to them, it was just not a gentleman's word" (Rose 1990: 47). In the jazz world, "funk" signalled a return to roots, and in line with its sexual connotation espoused a more relaxed, pleasurable and "groovy" approach to the music that emerged in contradistinction to "the coldness, complexity, and intellectualism introduced into the music by Bop, Cool, West Coast, and Third Stream jazz" (Keyes 2002: 41).

The term funk, like soul before it, would transcend its initial musical context, only to be re-adopted and re-adapted by those outside the jazz world.

Both terms were significant of an emergent "black" aesthetic, whose authenticity was derived from an organic, African-American derived aesthetic and argot. The terms funk and soul as musical descriptors offered an important distinction to white created music concepts such as rock 'n' roll and rhythm 'n' blues, and it was perhaps due to its exclusively "black" pedigree that made the term funk increasingly attractive to Brown, who took on the term "to denote an earthy and gritty sonority characterized specifically [to his] preachy vocal style and his horn and rhythm section's interlocking rhythmic 'grooves'" (ibid.).

Alternate theories on funk's etymology have speculated that funk's return to "roots" goes back a lot further than a movement in jazz. For instance, Robert Palmer cites the work of African arts scholar Robert Farris Thompson where the latter is to suggest:

> . . . that "funky" may derive from the Ki-Kongo *lu-fuki*, defined as "positive sweat." This is very close to the contemporary American usage, and Thompson notes that in present-day Africa, Ba-Kongo people use *lu-fuki* and the American "funky" synonymously – "to praise persons for the integrity of their art." Thus James Brown's celebrated admonition to "Make it funky now!" Certainly no one in rock or r and b has put more sweat into his performances than Soul Brother Number One. Add to this Ki-Kongo concept of "positive sweat" the Yoruba concept of *ashe*, or "cool" ("this is character," writes Thompson in Flash of the Spirit, "this is mystic coolness") and what have you got? "Cold Sweat"! (Palmer 1996: 239).

While the connection is uncanny, such etymological claims are, of course, moot. While previous studies on Brown have attempted to pursue the emergence of Brown's funk as a modern reiteration of a deeply African aesthetic, this "relationship" is drawn upon, perhaps, a little too indiscriminately. The major deficiency of this approach is that it fosters a lazy reductionism as it attempts to give the music a nominal ethnic identification which only tends to subsume commentary on funk's more immediate influences. A typical example of such essentialism can be found in the following quote from Vincent's *Funk*: "By turning rhythmic structure on its head, emphasizing the downbeat – the 'one' in a four beat bar – the Godfather kick-started a new pop trend and made a rhythmic connection with Africa at the same time" (Vincent 1996: 8).

Yet Brown's dislocation from any immediate connection to Africa escapes further problematization. Given his impoverished childhood and lack of education, one would hardly expect Brown to possess any consciousness of African musical forms; he had, of course, formulated his funk template long before he even visited that continent in the late 1960s. In fact, Brown has always adamantly denied any African lineage for his music, such as in this passage that appears in his 1986 autobiography:

> It's a funny thing about me and African music. I didn't even know it existed. When I got the consciousness of Africa and decided to see what my roots were, I thought I'd find out where my thing came from. My roots may be embedded in me and I don't know it, but when I went to Africa I didn't recognize anything that I had gotten from there (Brown and Tucker 1986: 221).

In fact, Brown's reluctance to identify with Africa has become the subject of some controversy, attributed to his fear of ethnicity. The apparent dichotomy in Brown's loyalties, according to Robert Farris Thompson, is "based on his fears of a compromise of his personal Southern Christianity" (Rose 1990: 126):

> "I know Brown thinks his Africanness could be a problem," adds Thompson. "He feels that, to admit it, he might have to give up his religion. But in the 1990s, misapprehensions like that will disappear. People are going to realize that to be a Baptist or an African Methodist Episcopalian in black America is automatically at the same time to have been practising, coded and creolized, the classical religions of the Kongo . . . James Brown . . . is already there, he was already blended. There is nothing here for him to lose. The Bakongo themselves welcomed the Catholic fathers and took on the cross of Jesus – because they saw similar, equal potency. So that is the cry of the future: the cry of the blues and the cry of James Brown and the cry of the whole Afro-Atlantic world!

To stop seeing each other as problems and realize these are equal potencies" (Thompson in Rose 1990: 128–29).

The Black Atlantic

Perhaps the prudent strategy is to not overplay the African lineage but instead to problematize it within the Afro-Atlantic context that Thompson has identified, a context perhaps better understood as the product of a *Black Atlantic* (1993) aesthetic. As argued in Paul Gilroy's seminal text, the Black Atlantic subject is *between* identities, a product of "routes" rather the "roots" (Gilroy 2004: 87), that results from African trans-Atlantic migration – enforced or otherwise. Rather than engage in discussion built around notions of Eurocentrism or Afrocentrism, Gilroy has instead conceived the Black Atlantic as an attempt to provide a theoretical vehicle for "an explicitly transnational and intercultural" approach (Gilroy 1993: 15) that might make sense of an ongoing transcultural exchange between Africa and the West. The focus on "routes" allows Gilroy to present the complexity of the pan-continental becoming of the Black Atlantic subject, rather than approach its theorization through a more simplistic, linear migratory pattern leading from Africa into the West. In this respect, a Black Atlantic music will emphasize the mutual becoming of both Africa and the new world as a result of the transcultural passages of the Black Atlantic subject:

> The pre-eminence of music within the diverse black communities of the Atlantic diaspora is itself an important element in their essential connectedness. But the histories of borrowing, displacement, transformation, and continual reinscription that the musical culture encloses are a living legacy that should not be reified in the primary symbol of the diaspora and then employed as an alternative to the recurrent appeal of fixity and rootedness (Gilroy 1993: 102).

In line with this move away from "fixity and rootedness" Gilroy's appeals for an "anti-anti-essentialist" approach that might be more appropriate for a discussion of "black music" that is not unduly hampered by the meta-commentary on relative ethicality (1993: 100). In support of this "anti-anti-essentialist" approach, Gilroy looks to musical examples that emerge from the

Black Atlantic and which exhibit "the syncretic complexity of black expressive cultures" (1993: 101). To demonstrate, he solicits examples as diverse as the Fisk Jubilee Singers, Jimi Hendrix and the Impressions (1993: 89–96) as representative of Black Atlantic subjects that might reflect its complex "circulatory systems" (1993: 88), the product of transnational movement rather than national origin. While Gilroy does in fact mention James Brown's music, it is only in passing (1993: 104–105), a pity, because I would argue that Brown's music is also suitably representative of such Black Atlantic syncreticism. While Brown does not have the same Black Atlantic pedigree, as, say, a peer such as Jimi Hendrix (1993: 93–94), he is still very much a product of this conceptual space.

On the most general level this might be found in terms of Brown's attempts to reconnect with Africa. His first visit was in March 1968, to Abidjan, Ivory Coast at the invitation of that country's government (G. Brown 1996: 155). He subsequently travelled to Zambia in 1970. The footage of Brown in Zaire in 1974 and Senegal in 1975 are captured on film for posterity. Yet his travels to the continent did little to assuage his reluctance to accede any African musical influence. "I went over there and I heard their thing, and I felt their thing. But I honestly hadn't heard their thing in mine," he told Cynthia Rose (Rose 1990: 126).

Yet Brown's relationship to "roots" came from the musical legacy of the church, a potent cultural intercessor. The Africa attributed to Brown's music might be heard to exude from the play of repetition and cut, inherent to the rapturous gospel style that had proven so attractive to Brown's funk template. It was this music that could be seen to have instilled in him the preeminence of non-chronological time, where repetition is part of the African DNA of his musical grooves.

Yet the "Brown finds Africa" account belies a deeper logical inconsistency; if the funk assemblage was so closely related to an African musical heritage, then why did this aesthetic emerge so discernibly from Brown's music and not one of his predecessors? Declaring Brown had some direct line to Africa doesn't really come close to clarifying this conundrum. My compulsion to frame Brown's work in terms of an "apprehension of a minor temporality" was to counteract some of the rather lazy ethnomusicological approaches to his work that I have previously encountered.

Perhaps what we are really accounting for is Brown's emphasis on the most discernible elements of the black aesthetic which, in turn, reinforced its difference. As I shall argue a little later in the chapter, Brown's great gift to music was his artistic naïvety, which is not a denigration of his contribution, but rather a celebration of his capacity to think without presupposition. Through sheer force of will, Brown proceeded to make music his way, often flaunting contemporary tastes in the process. Yes, he mediated a black aesthetic but one inspired with a plethora of influence. A potential rationale is that once Brown had exorcised his need for commercial acceptance he was free to experiment and recapitulate the more minimalist repetition of the gospel style that he had abandoned after 'Please, Please, Please'.

Using "the one" as anchor, it was this repetition that, from the mid-1960s onward, would discernibly set his funk music apart from the work of his contemporaries. Though no inventions emerge entirely from a vacuum. There were, of course, some important indications of funk to be witnessed before its formalization, examples that include 'I've Got Money' (1962) or 'Oh Baby Don't You Weep' (1964), the latter based on an older gospel song, 'Oh Mary Don't You Weep'. This track is, for example, one of the first of many of Brown's elongated jams that warranted two-part singles where a single title would take up both A *and* B-sides of the record.

Brown's music increasingly resisted both the form and function of the single as commodity form, and, by extension, the linearity of composition required to fit into this format; a singular composition through which the listener would be steered for a period lasting roughly two-and-a-half to three minutes. Brown's compositional methods increasingly rejected a linear and easily navigable trajectory that would maintain a traditional build-up to and exploitation of the hook/refrain. Brown's increasing reliance on groove, which would transmogrify into funk, pushed the nominal limits of the recorded medium, and reflected an emancipatory spirit much in keeping with the imminent conditions of a burgeoning civil rights Afro-America.

Papa's Got a Brand New Bag

Which is why Brown's 'Papa's Got a Brand New Bag' emerges as a significant expression of a minor language, and a revolutionary assemblage of difference. On the face of it, the song was simply a reiteration of the formula that would sustain a triumvirate of singles including 'Out of Sight' (1964) and 'I Got You (I Feel Good)' (1965), all of which were based on a simple twelve-bar form. Yet it was the groundbreaking approach to syncopation that differentiated these titles and, in the process, delivers to Brown a long sought-after international following. As Cliff White remarks in the liner notes to *Roots of a Revolution* (1988), these singles in particular would "introduce James Brown to a far greater audience than had previously been aware of his existence. Those who first heard Brown on 'Out Of Sight' wouldn't have realized that it sounded considerably different to any of his previous recordings and was released through different outlets to his previous R&B hits" (White 1989).

'Out of Sight' becomes the nominal beginning of Brown's "new breed" period – the neologistic expression appearing in 'Papa's Got a Brand New Bag' as constitutive of Brown's new musical approach. 'Out of Sight' also served as a prototype for 'Papa's Got a Brand New Bag'. The follow-up single, which again took on the twelve-bar form, would assert Brown's commitment to rhythmic change even more profoundly. Both rhythmically and lyrically, 'Papa's Got a Brand New Bag' was all minor code. While 'Out Of Sight' made use of vernacular, 'Papa' was steeped in the language of the streets. Brown's penchant for articulating idiom in a sometimes-impenetrable Southern accent, only served to accentuate the difference of this world to the many of the white teens who had begun buying Brown's records at this time. The commodity-driven encounter proved a vital cultural intermediary, unveiling to this demographic some hitherto invisible sections of American society.

While it is difficult to pinpoint exactly when Brown started to call this new formulation, funk, he was certainly beaten to the use of the term on record. That honour went to Dyke and the Blazers who put out 'Funky Broadway' (1967), perhaps more famously covered by Wilson Pickett in the same year. Brown also had a single with funk in the title that year, 'Funky Soul No.1' (1967), a rather obscure single that did not chart. Despite this new generic attribution, funk as genre truly arrived with the release of Brown's groundbreaking 'Cold Sweat' (1967):

> 'Cold Sweat' was almost completely divorced from other forms of popular music; soon Brown's lyrics had reduced themselves to free association, melody had virtually disappeared, the band (now under the direction of Pee Wee Ellis) featured two, and sometimes three, drummers in live performance to match its leader's ever-more-propulsive drive, and James's voice was strained to the breaking point – past it, in fact, as sometime during this period he was forced to abandon his characteristic scream for a succession of shrieks, whinnies, grunts, and emphatic Good God!s, with normal

speech reduced to a husky whisper that could only serve as a scarred warning to other singers (White in Guralnick 1986: 242–43).

By way of confirmation of this statement Jerry Wexler, the legendary Atlantic producer of Aretha Franklin and other soul stars, commented, "'Cold Sweat' deeply affected the musicians I knew . . . It just freaked them out. For a time, no one could get a handle on what to do next" (Wexler in Weinger and White 1991: 31). To quote Fred Wesley, who would himself would serve Brown on the cutting edge of funk in the 1970s: "Do you think you could have accepted a tune as radical as 'Cold Sweat' from a less bizarre artist?" (Wesley 2002: 302).

Prior to joining Brown's band, Wesley was not a fan of funk at all, and reportedly went out of his way to avoid playing tracks such as 'Cold Sweat' with his own group, because he thought them musically "ridiculous" (ibid.). His refusal to play 'Cold Sweat' climaxed in a near mutiny of his band:

> A few people had requested some of these songs, such as 'Cold Sweat' by James Brown. I had heard 'Cold Sweat' and was very unimpressed with it. It was not on par with the material we were playing. It only had one change, the words made no sense at all, and the bridge was musically incorrect. I wasn't about to abandon our upscale style and selection of music and sink to the level of a little honky-tonk sissy singer and sound like every other band up and down the pike (ibid.).

Within a year, Wesley would be one of Brown's accomplices in the production of this "bizarre" music.

The 'Illogic' of Innovation

While James Brown's pioneering music would continue to attract great critical acclaim, it was not widely acknowledged that his own musicians were less than effusive about his "bizarre" approach to composition. Brown's musically "educated" band members have often expressed the view that his prototype funk compositions were simplistic and unsophisticated and therefore not to be taken very seriously. This view is strikingly borne out in Fred Wesley's recent book *Hit Me, Fred: Recollections of a Sideman* (2002) in which Brown's former bandleader provides the most comprehensive insight to date into the trials and tribulations of working with the "Godfather of Soul." Wesley was among the core of abundantly talented former jazz players – Alfred "Pee Wee" Ellis, Maceo Parker, Waymond Reed were others – of Brown's premier late 1960s–early 1970s troupes. Prior to their recruitment into Brown's band, these musicians were aspirant be-boppers. As ex-James Brown bandleader, "Pee Wee" Ellis would later say, "he was some other stuff for me; I'd been studying Sonny Rollins" (Rose 1990: 51). This "other stuff" a formative "funk," in which Ellis was instrumental in realizing, took on its form through the notoriously "idiosyncratic" approach to composition that Wesley would subsequently lament:

> Mr. Brown would sometimes come to the gig early and have what we call a "jam", where we would have to join in with his fooling around on the organ. This was painful for anyone who had ever thought of playing jazz. James Brown's organ playing was just good enough to fool the untrained ear, and so bad that it made real musicians sick on the stomach (Wesley 2002: 110–11).

This sentiment is echoed by long-time Brown stalwart and drumming legend, John "Jabo" Starks, who recalls:

> James would come in and get the sticks and sit down behind the drums and say, "well, this is the way I want you to play it." And you still haven't figured out which way he wanted it to go. Your best answer was, "'OK, gotcha Mr. Brown'." So you'd sit right back down and play what you were playing anyway. Because he never really played! Hey, man, I'm being honest, James did not play anything! He even wanted to fool around with the guitar! And he couldn't! (Gladstone, Simins and Starks 1997: 43).

Brown's musical shortcomings, coupled with his notoriously autocratic style of leadership, made for a difficult gig. By all reports, his despotism often made for a demeaning and debilitating experience and, from time to time, his musicians would avenge such maltreatment by belittling their employer's musical ability. An example of note from Wesley's book involves the antics of former trumpeter Waymond Reed, whom Wesley cites as one of the most consistently confrontational members of the group:

> In the dressing room, he [Reed] took out his horn and for hours and more hours played parts of Count Basie's *Shiny Stockings*, pausing between licks to laugh real loud and say stuff like, "'That's real music," not the honky-tonk stuff we have to play on this gig (Wesley 2002: 105).

The musicians' collective frustration was compounded by the fact that playing popular music was a far more lucrative proposition than was generally offered in the jazz world. Indeed, the more prominent members of the James Brown bands looked upon their tenure with Brown as a stepping-stone to a higher calling. The cantankerous Waymond Reed, for example, went on to play with Max Roach and the Count Basie Orchestra, and was later joined by Fred Wesley, while "Pee Wee" Ellis would go on to assume the directorship of Van Morrison's band. Harbouring such musical ambition, the musicians' animosity towards Brown's restrictive musical vision is less than surprising. To add further insult to injury, Brown would subsequently bask in the acclaim afforded his revolutionary funk style, despite the fact that he did not even understand basic music theory. As Wesley explains:

> Simple things like knowing the key would be a big problem for James. So, when James would mouth out some guitar part, which might or might not have had anything to do with the actual song being played, Jimmy or Country [former James Brown guitarists] would have to attempt to play it simply because James was still in charge. We all had to pretend that we knew what James was talking about. Nobody ever said, "'That's ridiculous'" or "'You don't know what you're talking about'" (2002: 97).

Among the prerequisites for the job of band leader was an ability to successfully translate the boss's grunts and groans (for the uninitiated, think an early version of "beatboxing") into releasable product. As "Pee Wee" Ellis informs the viewer of *Lenny Henry Hunts the Funk* (1992), Brown would merely grunt certain "feels" and then demand that the current band leader translate them into musical notation. A brief snippet of Brown grunting the beat of 'Cold Sweat' can be heard on the 1996 compilation, James Brown, *Foundations of Funk: a Brand New Bag 1964–1969* (Polygram, 1996). In glaring contrast to the musical prowess of his esteemed alumni, the only virtuosity Brown is known to have displayed (his organ-playing is a source of contention) was his ability to mouth sounds to his bandleaders:

> I kept on putting together James's hums and grunts and groans, and making music out of them, no matter how stupid I thought it was. I began to take pride in my ability to make something out of anything or something out of nothing or something out of any combination of things. I gave James no trouble when he laid out formats to songs. I simply took the orders as he gave them, never questioning, and worried about how to make it happen later. But sometimes I had trouble getting the musicians to accept such unorthodox patterns as readily as I did. I had to argue, convince, trick, and manipulate guys into doing all kinds of unusual things (Wesley 2002: 158–59).

From this perspective, one could hardly blame Wesley for believing Brown's music to be a great embarrassment, especially as he would find himself having to negotiate respected studio musicians to play this "silly music" (ibid.). All in all, Brown's ex-employees often expressed disdain for their association with his music. Wesley, for instance, has spoken of his embarrassment over the compositions with which he was involved, even though they were among Brown's most popular titles:

> I was getting credit for a lot of the music, as most people were looking at the music as James's and mine together. While I admit that I did most of the implementation of the music, the concepts were practically all his. It didn't sit right with me to be getting credit for music, especially since, frankly, I didn't think it was all that great . . . I got this sick feeling when anyone told me how great 'Pass The Peas' was (2002: 172).

Such disillusioning accounts of Brown's unorthodox approach to composition raise some intriguing questions. How did Brown manage to maintain the level of agency required not only to direct such talent, but also to synthesize such differences of musical opinion into the cohesive and enduring influence on popular music it has since become? The James Brown story points to an interesting inconsistency in the supposed correlation between hands-on pragmatism and its relation to actual musical agency, providing, instead, a tale of ruthless determination victorious over traditionally recognized "ability." How might we begin to account for this tremendous innovation achieved by a man who, by all accounts, could barely play an instrument?

The Idiot

To analyse Brown's inimitable compositional processes most fruitfully, I would suggest that an application of Deleuze's concept of the "Idiot" might be beneficial. This is not, it should be said at the outset, to speak ill of the "Godfather of Soul." On the contrary, I will attempt to illustrate how a certain type of naïvety was necessary to realize one of music's most creative forces. For one of Brown's most enduring gifts to contemporary music practice was his willing embrace of "illogic" in the face of a dogmatic image of musical thought, a quality shared with the Deleuzean Idiot of *Difference and Repetition* (1994).

The Idiot character plays a pivotal role in Deleuze's quest for a way of conceiving a philosophy undaunted by the presuppositions of a "dogmatic" image of thought. This "dogmatic" image of thought can be broadly perceived as any institutionally dominant form of thinking, or that propensity to reinforce already dominant modes of thought. It is in "The Image of Thought" chapter of *Difference and Repetition* that Deleuze develops the Idiot as a type of perspectival character or what he and Guattari would later term a "conceptual persona" (Deleuze and Guattari 1994: 61–63). The Idiot will ask "what would it mean to start philosophy 'undogmatically,' or with an image that secretes no illusions of transcendence" (Rajchman 2000: 36). Our rather generalized understanding of "common sense" provides a prime example of a dogmatic image of thought in so far as it proposes a uniform objectivity and rationality by default, and one thus limiting to our perception of difference. This is why Deleuze and Guattari will champion the artist's naïvety as a necessary force in dispensing with the overwhelming institutional and dogmatic power of a generalized common sense.

We should consider the idea that all artists are Idiots, then, in the sense that their creativity depends on flouting "common sense," to otherwise wilfully plunge the world into the relative chaos of unorthodoxy. Perhaps it was Brown's resistance to the orthodox way of making music that would appeal to the egalitarian musical outlook of a new generation of musical Idiots, those DJs and dance music producers of the future, who would so enthusiastically sample and synthesize Brown's refrains into new and unforeseen musical connections.

It is difficult to bring these new connections to bear if one is busy adhering to the presuppositions of orthodoxy. This is why the celebration of artists, philosophers and scientists who attempt to think without presupposition is a recurrent theme throughout Deleuze's work. The Idiot's repudiation of the presupposition of orthodoxy gives way to a necessary faith in difference: manifest in chance, and stumbled upon through experimentation. This naïve faith in difference obviously requires a particular audacity, and James Brown most certainly possessed such a quality, as Wesley has testified in the preceding series of recollections.

Brown fans are rather less likely to judge the man's apparent lack of instrumental proficiency so harshly, and his idiosyncratic musicianship is of course acceptable to many ears. In fact Brown's musical talent was of a multi-instrumental capability: there was his aforementioned penchant for organ, but his other notable instrumental contributions to his records include the more than passable drumming on several early recordings, including the well-known 1962 hit version of 'Night Train' (1962). The verdicts of Brown's peers may thus appear overly harsh as they were judging him within the domain of the "real" musician. In spite of such criticisms, Brown's organ or piano accompaniment can be inspirational precisely because of this very incongruity. Instead of trying to maintain a distinction between "good" and "bad" musicianship, we need to recognize how this concept of the "real" musician itself functions as a constricting presupposition and one that can never be conducive to musical innovation. Hence my argument that a key part of Brown's ultimate legacy was his frank ambivalence towards such a distinction.

It was an ambivalence that Deleuze shared, renowned as he was for his own naïve perspective on the history of philosophy. Issuing a challenge to a philosophy in which thought has a "natural" orientation towards truth, and where notions of common logic and reason will necessarily elaborate this truth, Deleuze was sceptical about the validity of any will-to-truth that implies an *a priori* nature of thought, with an assumed teleology, meaning and logic.

This is why using Deleuze to approach James Brown's music is not so strange a strategy. My own initial attraction to Brown's music was because of its flagrantly unconventional nature: some of it, in fact, seems downright bizarre even today, but even more so, when contrasted with the work of his soul music contemporaries. Brown's subversive approach to composition would most effectively channel the dynamism of the civil-rights era and catalyse it into musical aesthetic. The apparent formal simplicity of funk was key to its vital territorial presence, driven, as it was, by an ensemble approach much at odds with the individualistic virtuosity of the modern jazz styles beloved by his musicians. In this respect, Brown's music can be seen to have gravitated towards a "minor becoming" in which, as Deleuze and Guattari tell us, "everything takes on a collective value" (Deleuze and Guattari 1986: 17).

Hence it would be fair to maintain that Brown's collective approach to composition, and his tendency to treat his band as a rhythm machine, were more reflective of the image of thought that underlies "minor becoming" than that of the individual agency that drove the ideal of the virtuoso still prevalent in, say, the be-bop jazz movement of his time.

Brown's minor approach to musical composition required a philosophical leap and one that could only result from the unregimented perspective of the naïve, or of those minorities who have yet to master and majorize a language:

> talent isn't abundant . . . there are no possibilities for an individuated enunciation that would belong to this or that "master" and that could be separated from a collective enunciation. Indeed, scarcity of talent is in fact beneficial and allows the conception of something other than a literature of masters; what each author says individually already constitutes a common action, and what he or she says or does is necessarily political, even if others aren't in agreement (Deleuze and Guattari 1986: 17).

While Brown was often the nominal "author" of his work, funk was dependent on an ensemble of interlocking grooves woven together with formidable intricacy. This collective approach, in turn, would begin to influence the shift away from virtuoso performances towards more abstract forms of composition – such as the abstraction that is audible in some of Brown's most nebulous arrangements, as in the following anecdote recounted by Mike D of the Beastie Boys:

> Adam was talking to this guy about the song *The Payback* by James Brown. And the guy was trying to say that the guitar was playing nothing. But see, I figure, well, if the guitar is playing nothing, then that means the entire band is playing nothing. But, then, that's the best playing ever on, like, any song. And they're all playing nothing (Beastie Boys and Heatley 1999: 50).

Brown's abstract approach to composition was a product of a commitment to difference. It would influence, in turn, those musicians who similarly prized difference over orthodoxy, and who were committed to a musical *becoming* through a willingness to *forget* the rules. The Miles Davis of the late 1960s, who was listening to Brown with interest, would do just that.

In 1968, Davis publicly declared, "My favourite music is Stockhausen, *Tosca* and James Brown" (Werner 2000: 139), and funk would impel Davis to redefine his own approach to composition, as Bob Belden recounts in the liner notes to Davis's *On the Corner* (1972):

> Davis had moved closer and closer to the funk-based sound of James Brown and Sly Stone, and the musicians he hired began to reflect this direction in his tastes. The first musician Davis would hire was Michael Henderson, an accomplished funk bass player. Henderson's "locked in" bass grooves simplified the ground that Davis wanted to walk on. Davis' sound headed to the bottom of the band (Belden in Werner 2000: 139).

As documented on albums such as *Bitches Brew* (1971) and *On the Corner* (1972), Davis's "radical" turn in the early 1970s was marked by this stylistic shift to an emphasis on groove rather than solos:

> Miles followed his interest in Brown's experimental funk
> "down into a deep African thing, a deep African-American
> groove, with a lot of emphasis on drums and rhythm, and
> not on individual solos." When Miles added Brown's funk, Sly
> Stone's rhythmically innovative soul, and Hendrix's rock to
> his musical mix, the results were spectacular (ibid.)

Given Davis's attention to Brown's work at this time, there is an acute irony in the fact that a man who was maligned among his own band for his apparent musical ineptitude should end up influencing the very musicians they most admired. While Brown's personnel were occupied with dreams of being recognized as "proper" musicians, Brown's innovations were having direct aesthetic implications for the evolution of jazz itself and, in the process, helping to render any dogmatic image of the genre anachronistic.

For instance, in *The Black Atlantic*, Paul Gilroy discusses the feud that erupted between Miles Davis and the neo-classicist style of Wynton Marsalis (Gilroy 1993: 97). According to this anecdote, it would appear that Davis maintained a long-term feud with Marsalis because of the latter's adherence to an *image* of jazz. Davis would, for instance, mock Marsalis's adherence to the anachronistic jazz aesthetic, something that the latter would emulate right down to its dress code (ibid.). Meanwhile jazz traditionalists greeted Davis's experimentation with an indignant reproach as if the music had represented some sort of backward step by succumbing to electricity (Lerner [dir.] 2004). While one could understand Marsalis's pride in this most influential African-American art form and his celebration of it, it also says something about the nature of art – Davis is an "artist" because he would never live in the past at the expense of the present. Paul Gilroy will also criticize Marsalis's essentialism as indicative of "[t]he fragmentation and subdivision of black music into an ever increasing proliferation of styles and genres which makes a nonsense of this polar opposition between progress and dilution" (Gilroy 1993: 96).

In fact, I would contend that Brown gave musicians such as Davis a way out of their own musical habits, inducing in them a similar "idiocy." Davis, too, is renowned for his propensity for reinvention and for becoming – a reputation forged through wilful plunges into the "chaosmos," or that "consistent chaos" (Deleuze and Guattari 1994: 208) of life which forces one to come up with concepts to make sense of it (Werner 2000: 139). To take the plunge into the chaosmos, then, requires a certain naïvety, as it is only the truly naïve who will experiment rather than accept conditions "as they are."

For this reason, art's minor status, established through the production of affects or becomings, will be understood in contradistinction to the concept of opinion as the organizational property of the majority (Deleuze and Guattari 1994: 146). As Deleuze and Guattari write in *What is Philosophy?* "[t]he essence of opinion is will to majority and already speaks in the name of majority" (ibid.) and they explain this through the example of the competition which asks its audience to provide its opinion but where you can only "win," "if you say the same as the majority of those participating" (ibid.). To break from this stultifying majoritarian world of opinion we require that character who is not out to win any such competitions, the character that Deleuze refers to as the work of the "seer and no longer of the agent" (Deleuze 1989: 126) whose very *innocence* of the dominant constructions of truth will, unwittingly perhaps, set its falsification in place.

Brown as 'Seer'

Embracing the "illogical" is always the result of a deep dissatisfaction with the restrictions of "common sense" and its stultifying impact on the possibilities of becoming. In this respect, being "illogical" involves a belief in the world and all of its possibilities, rather than filtering it through the perception of what *is*. Such a submission to the world is available for those seeking an alternative to a majoritarian political solution. The naïvety involved is a characteristic of the seer, who will emerge from the shadow of the movement-image's agency, to otherwise affirm the potential of immanence by submitting to it. The seer is therefore a type of "spiritual automaton," in that seers are totally immersed in the present moment of the world's becoming:

> The spiritual automaton is in the psychic situation of the seer, who sees better and further than he can react, that is, think. Which, then, is the subtle way out? To believe, not in a different world, but in a link between man and the world, in love or life, to believe in this as in the impossible, the unthinkable, which none the less cannot but be thought: "something possible, otherwise I will suffocate." It is this belief that makes the unthought the specific power of thought, through the absurd, by virtue of the absurd (Deleuze 1989: 169–70).

This passage from Deleuze's *Cinema 2* may further illuminate Brown's own seer-like qualities, which brought to the world such previously unthought musical concepts as funk, or "the one." Such a wilful submission to the "chaosmos" shakes up the banal reiteration of musical habit.

Indeed, the perspective of the Idiot may be what ultimately distinguishes the great artist from those who are simply technically proficient. In this respect the Idiot will show us

> not only that philosophical thought is unlearned, but also that it is free in its creations not when everyone agrees or plays by the rules, but on the contrary, when what the rules and who the players are is not given in advance, but instead emerges along with the new concepts created and the new problems posed (Rajchman 2000: 38).

In presenting my defence of Brown's autodidactic musical pursuits, I should add that I am not necessarily celebrating "poor" musicianship nor preferring a lack of training to working within a tradition. Nevertheless, the point is that it is difficult, perhaps more difficult, to work outside a tradition than it is to work within one and to maintain the sort of acceptance that Brown enjoyed. In fact, the factor that sets Brown apart from his peers is precisely his courage to affirm difference in the face of ridicule. This is the leap one takes in order to become-minor, assisted only by a resolve to believe in the world, but without maintaining an adherence to common sense. Such a deliberate embrace of minority requires the removal of an overarching rule of judgement that mediates a dogmatic image of thought. In the process, fresh possibilities necessarily begin to open up.

Perhaps what makes an artist "cutting edge" is an ability to apprehend a minor temporality and develop it accordingly. The affirmation of creative thought requires casting aside self-consciousness based upon dogged adherence to one's supposed identity. Perhaps we can say that this is how stars become parodies – they lose that innocent sense of invention or, as Deleuze would say, that thought without an image. Instead it becomes thought based on the habit of capitulating to dogma. In such circumstances, we will always require the disruptive force of an Idiot, to inspire those naïve revolutions in thought that allows thinking itself to proceed.

In turn, we could say that the great artist is one who is willing to undermine the notion of the "common sense" of his or her own position. We have also learnt that the movements – social or individual – best enabled by what we broadly categorize as music can sometimes be initiated by those who would be indifferent to accepting the role of "musician." As hip-hop producer Hank Shocklee once remarked: "Who says you have to be a musician to make music? We might respond that we don't require a musician to make music, all we require is a missing people, or a 'people to come'" (Deleuze and Guattari 1988: 345). As Deleuze comments in *Cinema 2*, art "must take part in this task: not that of addressing a people, which is presupposed already there, but of contributing to the invention of a people" (Deleuze 1989: 217):

> It's the greatest artists (rather than populist artists) who invoke a people, and find they "lack a people" ... Artists can only invoke a people, their need for one goes to the very heart of what they're doing, it's not their job to create one, and they can't. Art is resistance: it resists death, slavery, infamy, shame. But a people can't worry about art. How is a people created, through what terrible suffering? When a people's created, it's through its own resources, but in a way that links up with something in art ... or links up art to what it lacked (Deleuze 1995: 174).

As Deleuze and Guattari contend in *What is Philosophy?*, the fields of philosophy, science and the arts invoke their own particular methods to plunge their audience into the chaosmos (Deleuze and Guattari 1994: 202). In this respect, the role of the artist is to "[bring] back from the chaos varieties that no longer constitute a reproduction of the sensory in the organ but set up a being of the sensory, a being of sensation, on an anorganic plane of composition that is able to restore the infinite" (Deleuze and Guattari 1994: 202–203). Thus the artwork does not seek to represent a coherent vision, but rather gives access to the diverse connections of affect behind it. In fact, it is impossible to *represent* the experience of the chaosmos because the experience will always be too overwhelming. The artists will always necessarily find themselves incapable of relating the full power of its intensity. The lesson is to continue to experiment.

Viewed in such terms, the music of James Brown was tantamount to a series of scientific experiments into what made people move, where the act of movement itself might be perceived a series of relative connections with the chaosmos. In setting up the possibility for, and drive within, this new experience of movement-connection, Brown would return to the essence of the nature of being minor and providing an art "positively charged with the role and function of collective, and even revolutionary, enunciation" (Deleuze and Guattari 1986: 17). A different kind of collectivity was the ultimate "message" of Brown's music. Yet, Brown has quite openly testified that the dawn of funk was stumbled upon rather than dreamed in advance:

> "Funk was not a project", he growls. "It happened as part of my ongoing thing. In 1965, I changed from the upbeat to the downbeat. Simple as that, really. I wasn't going for some known sound, I was aimin' for what I could *hear*. 'James Brown Anticipation' I'd call it. You see, the thing was *ahead*" (Rose 1990: 59).

True to the sheer pragmatic function of the Idiot, Brown did not mistakenly attribute presuppositions of intent to his work or align it with some transcendental project that would undermine its very newness. One cannot try to capture the future – it must be allowed to become in its own unpredictable and often illogical ways. In short, Brown catalysed the funk assemblage – even if somewhat accidentally and experimentally – rather than invented it via some grand vision.

The fact of the matter is that Brown did not restrict his musical activities to funk composition – even if it was the bold originality of this style that would eventually secure his place in musical history. Indeed, for all of the cutting-edge innovation of his funk years, we cannot extricate Brown's sustained effort to model himself as a crooner and a serious interpreter of "standard" in the style of a Nat King Cole or Frank Sinatra. It is important to take Brown's eclectic musical tastes into account, because it is the very schizophrenic nature of his albums (in particular, those of the 1960s and 1970s) that are indicative of the disparate audiences to which he was attempting to appeal. However, despite such attempts throughout the years to present himself in the guise of the mainstream-friendly crooner, Brown would never have any kind of sustained success with the white audience in the sense of gaining the crossover visibility of a Ray Charles, or even a Motown, despite his superstar status among African-Americans. It is Brown's comparatively marginal and, as I have argued, "minor" status that is so enticing to those other minor musicians of electronic dance music and sampling cultures today. For these musicians are beneficiaries of Brown's own eschewal of musical orthodoxy based upon opinion and judgement. As Deleuze and Guattari write: "the struggle with chaos is only the instrument of a more profound struggle against opinion, for the misfortune of people comes from opinion" (Deleuze and Guattari 1994: 206). As we have learnt, Brown was not the type of performer to give in to opinion; rather, he had the Idiot's instinct for new orientations. As Wesley would recount in an earlier interview with Brown's biographer, Cynthia Rose:

> He has no real musical skills . . . yet he could hold his own onstage with any jazz virtuoso – because of his guts. Can you understand that? James Brown cannot play drums at all. But he would sit down on drums and get that look on his face like he's playin' 'em and you would just play along with him. Organ – he cannot play organ at all. A guitar's not an instrument you can bullshit on, you got to really know how to play a guitar. And I've seen him pick up a guitar and go #'£#'%' (sic) and look at you just like he's playin' it, you dig? (Rose 1990: 86).

Brown, as "Idiot," could not, or would not, uphold the "common-sense" image of thought. Nothing new can come from the appeal to a common sense predicated on the fact that "everybody knows" – "everybody knows you don't play a guitar like that!" Brown's music offers a pragmatic response embodying a resounding "says who?" Such pragmatism demonstrates the embrace of difference-in-itself – one that is necessary for any form of becoming.

Thought without Image

It is with becoming in mind that Deleuze makes plain his preference for the naïve thinker, citing the fact that it is only the truly naïve who can forget the constructed truths of the past and allow the forces of creation to emerge. We have also seen that this requires dispensing with the dogmatic image of thought, the presuppositions of common sense that restrict creative thought or difference-for-itself. It is in pursuit of such difference, or the overturning of the intuitive or "common sense" image of thought, that Deleuze champions "thought without image" (Deleuze 1994: 167) over the dogmatic image of thought. Deleuze further describes this "thought without image" as the pursuit of dangerous thought, because its object is no less than the vast chaosmos of difference-in-itself. This is *becoming-thought*, rather than inherited logic:

> The thought which is born in thought, the act of thinking which is neither given by innateness nor presupposed by reminiscence but engendered in its genitality, is a thought without image. But what is such a thought, and how does it operate in the world? (Deleuze 1994: 167).

Brown's music provides a convincing demonstration of how such "thought without image" is fundamental to new conceptual syntheses and that the *proper* way is not always conducive to progress. In fact, it is infeasibility that often becomes innovation in retrospect. On the point of Brown's musical deficiencies, Cynthia Rose posits:

> During the 1960s and early 70s, Brown's touch seemed so certain it dazzled new recruits as much as his towering ego bruised them. How did he – a man who relied on "real" musicians completely to implement his ideas – pick and choose his accomplices with such unwavering success? Pee Wee Ellis says he had "an inner ear." Ellis drums a beringed finger on the desk before him and savours the very words. "James has this instant ability, this basic mother-wit, which allowed him to apprehend a certain combination of things. And he could get close enough to accomplishing the spirit of it himself to figure 'if I can get this close, I can PUSH it the rest of the way'" (Rose 1990: 60).

Brown's alumni have retrospectively assessed the success of funk with a sense of incredulity, if only because it was not actually supposed to *work*, musically. However, the fact that it *did*, provided a lesson in creativity that the "learned" musicians in the band, such as Fred Wesley, were quick to acknowledge:

> "I've got to give James credit," says Wesley, "because he allowed me to be creative – he made it possible for me to be ultra-creative. Take a tune like *Doin' It to Death* (in 1973). I would never, ever, in my wildest imagination have thought of doin' something like that. But him givin' me a basic idea caused me to create that. It's my creation, but it's what he gave me to create with. He would give you these little, unrelated elements, sometimes not even musical, and say 'make something out of it'" (Rose 1990: 92–93).

Despite Wesley's criticisms of Brown, it must be pointed out that he is not one given to sour grapes and retains a balanced and ultimately sanguine perspective throughout his memoirs. As Brown's autocratic style made for an often rocky period of tenure, Wesley is conciliatory when he describes his former boss's inimitable depth of passion, which he says brought to the music a new level of energy and enabled it to "[take] on a new power" (Wesley 2002: 107).

Brown's challenge to Wesley illustrates that judgement about proper musicianship can ultimately hinder conceptual progress. We have seen Deleuze's championing of the Idiot's naïvety as a vital force for the creation of the new. However, there may be a darker side to the Idiot in all of this. The Idiot's disregard of the "proper" way to think reflects a blatant disregard of protocol that permeates every aspect of life. For this reason, Deleuze has suggested that the Idiot's instincts for ruthless survival can be perceived as cruel and callous – criticisms that have been similarly levelled at Brown:

> It is a question of someone – if only one – with the necessary modesty not managing to know what everybody knows, and modestly denying what everybody is supposed to recognise. Someone who neither allows himself to be represented nor wishes to represent anything. Not an individual endowed with good will and a natural capacity for thought, but an individual full of ill will that does not manage to think, either naturally or conceptually. Only such an individual is without presuppositions (Deleuze 1994: 130).

Deleuze's championing of such "immoral" characters as the Idiot has led his critics to accuse him of appearing to be apologist for this coldness and "indifference" (Lechte 1994: 104). Yet the main point for Deleuze is that the concept of judgement itself is the problem, if only because judgement is based on the reiteration of presuppositions and thus is not conducive to becoming. What is good for becoming is a necessary indifference to dogma that offers liberation from oppressive regimes of thought. This is the sort of naïve thought which we have attributed to Brown. Although not completely excusing callous behaviour, the "ill will" attributed to the Idiot is often inextricable from conceptual innovation.

So while it is lamentable that Brown treated his musicians so poorly, this "ill will" was also part and parcel of the sheer force of will required to transform musical concepts into belief. In this respect Brown's musical quest is concomitant with Deleuze's qualification that, ". . . in the most pressing situations, *The Idiot* feels the need to see the terms of a problem which is more profound than the situation, and even more pressing" (Deleuze 1989: 128). Having experienced the worst of the African-American experience, Brown had long inhabited a particularly limiting "world." That he foisted an alternative musical reality upon the shoulders of his peers was because his life, and perhaps by extension, that of a broader African-American society at the time, literally depended on it.

Via his particular affective strategies, Brown was redefining what it meant to be human at a time when the political processes of a world that appeared to be anything but human, or as neo-realist director, Roberto Rosselini was said to proclaim: ". . . the less human the world is, the more it is the artist's duty to believe and produce belief in a relation between man and the world" (Deleuze 1989: 170). Brown might be seen as exemplary here as he tried to push the boundaries of what a body could do "between man and the world," at a time when there were so many of these boundaries in a segregated American society. Unlike the more orthodox soul compositions of the mid-1960s, Brown seized this sense of minority, perhaps some of the monotony and the repetition of the imminent existential circumstances and gave them a tangible musical expression. The catalyst for Brown's aesthetic break might be seen as a response to the intolerable circumstances which produced it.

While the intolerable might, in some cases, reflect the truly catastrophic, it is similarly constitutive of the banality of the everyday (Deleuze and Guattari 1994: 171). As Deleuze has written in *Cinema 2: The Time-Image*:

> For it is not in the name of a better or truer world that thought captures the intolerable in this world, but, on the contrary, it is because this world is intolerable that it can no longer think a world or think itself. The intolerable is no longer a serious injustice, but the permanent state of a daily banality. Man is not himself a world other than the one in which he experiences the intolerable and feels himself trapped (Deleuze 1989: 169–70).

Such intolerable, daily banality was perhaps characteristic of the lives of a significant number of African-Americans in the 1960s, and who invested their hopes for social change within the "grand narrative" logic of the soul era (a logic that might be found, for instance, in the teleological projection implicit to the refrains of 'We Shall Overcome'). The term "grand narrative" is attributed to philosopher, Jean François Lyotard, who famously argued in his groundbreaking, *The Postmodern Condition: A Report on Knowledge* (1984), that postmodernism's cynicism of the historical narrative was the result of the decline in modernism's teleological and inherently progressive view of the world. It is the intolerable effects of World War II, for instance, which promoted this postmodern cynicism, just as the effects of that war are similarly responsible for the shift from movement to time in Deleuze's *Cinema* books.

Now Say Something

While the intolerable of the soul era will assume critical mass with the assassination of Dr. Martin Luther King, even prior to the symbolic magnitude of this tragedy, the intolerable conditions of the everyday marked the lives for the many minorities who looked to the civil-rights movement for change. If Afro-America had established its presence through the soul aesthetic, then some critics expected the performers to make the most of this new-found visibility to *say* something. For example, in *Black Talk* (1995 [1971]), Ben Sidran attacked the often deceptive political content of many soul songs, prompting his comment that the genre's frivolous nature was its major deficiency: "For all its clamor, the 'soul' movement was, at bottom, not a *serious* challenge to Western conventions at all. Although it had had serious implications in terms of a challenge to the dominant Puritan ethic, the music itself was rarely more than party music" (Sidran 1995: 133). Sidran's assessment is a good example, however, of the grand, and majoritarian, political gesture, and perhaps discounts musical presence as its own political contribution. As Mark Anthony Neal will later write, it was as *party music* that soul music had the ability to "[challenge] the prevailing logic of white supremacy and segregation in many ways that were discomforting to some, regardless of race or ethnicity" (Neal 2002: 4).

While Sidran makes an exception for Brown's music in his criticism of soul, it is also fair to say that a song like 'Papa's Got a Brand New Bag', for example, does not, at least on the surface, *appear* to say much at all. Little more than a check-list of dance moves, the record might be regarded by some as nothing less than insipid. Yet its real political potency was based on its "rendering visible" of previously invisible sections of America, ameliorating the resistance to majoritarian narrative as it experiments with affectively inspired creation of new territories. The political power of his work is not necessarily achieved by what it attempts to "say" – in fact lyricism might become mere rhetoric or dogma – but, rather, asserts its presence by using rhythm to pursue affectively inspired strategies of expression and becoming. In this respect, what took Brown beyond the strictures of the soul aesthetic was that he could give *the body* a new emphasis, and, through funk, emphasize the presence of the minority body as an inextricable element of its aesthetic.

This is why a central argument of this book is that Brown's greatest statements were always delivered musically rather than as a lyrical narrative. To try and understand the revolutionary impact of the music in terms of narrative is of negligible importance. The full "message" – the apprehension of a new minor temporality of becoming – is derived from the power of the music's rhythms, in particular the shift to "the one" that drove his new anthem, 'Papa's Got a Brand New Bag' and would bolster his hits into the future. As Brown would write in his recent, second autobiography, "'the one' was not just a new kind of beat; it was a statement of race, of force, of stature, of stride. It was the aural equivalent of standing tall and saying *Here I am*, of marching with strength rather than tiptoeing with timidity" (Brown and Eliot 2005: 72–73). Hence the message was not so much to be heard in what Brown was saying, but rather the way that he was saying it. Brown's next single and biggest hit, 'I Got You (I Feel Good),' again not a particularly overt political gesture on the surface, is given a new power of audacity, as he dares to "Feel Good," during a time when African-Americans were not expected to do so, and, if they did, were probably best keeping it to themselves lest they court the advances of some indiscriminate lynch mob.

In short, the political power of Brown's music was its challenge "deal with me" rather than to plead for "respect." As Brown would later sing "I don't want nobody to give me nothin', open up the door I'll get it myself . . . don't give me integration, give me truth, communication" (Brown 1970). One need only to heed the power of the live version of 'I Don't Want Nobody to Give Nothing' that appears on the *Sex Machine* album – one of the most incessant attacks on a single chord ever to be heard on record. Every downbeat on "the one" is signalled by a single sustained guitar chord, most likely by Alphonso "Country" Kellum, acting as the left hand jab, and with a fast Jimmy Nolen "chicken scratch" coming in from behind, providing the motion and the fancy footwork. When it comes time to deliver on the chin, Clyde or Jabo would then slam the equivalent of a vicious right on the snare on every second and fourth beat. Boom-Bap, Boom-Bap, Boom-Bap. Music that sent its audience into spontaneous bouts of air boxing. This is funk as the aural equivalent of a prize fight, and Brown's music was perpetually buoyant, through the incessant, almost violent, musical rallies in which he took hits from the various instruments, Brown might scream, wail, fall to his knees – but just as his trademark caped performance has indicated since the late 1950s, he never hit the canvas. As entered into historical record in 'Say It Loud! I'm Black and I'm Proud' (1968), Brown "would die on his feet rather than live on his knees." Repetition was the key, and Brown's incessant incantation affected an overwhelming sense of presence. Whether consciously or not, Brown was giving his audience lessons in how such a severe musically driven violence might sustain an audience who were hard pressed to engage in a more corporeal one. These calculated and precise musical attacks were all leveraged off of "the one."

An Expedient Production of Territory

There is nothing like a drum to mobilize a people, and the apparent "simplicity" of funk's melodic structure accommodated a more expedient production of territory. In short, the music's rhythmic predictability implored within those in earshot a rather pressing need for bodily movement. As Nelson George would remark in his *Death of Rhythm and Blues*, leaving space in the music for dance was intrinsic to funk's composition (George 1988: 102), tailored as it was for affective connection. Funk was so effective at the time precisely because it had successfully elevated rhythmic complexity to the level of attention once reserved for melodic and harmonic concerns, and

Brown dedicated himself to stripping the music down to rhythmic essentials accordingly. This approach is evident, for example, on the 1967 track, 'Get It Together', where Brown exhorts "don't play so much!" Brown would later explain this approach to Gerri Hirshey:

> I tried the heavy approach two or three times, and every time I tried, I'd get stopped. Just have to keep coming back and simplifying it. It's a funny thing. You make a little three-finger chord on the guitar and they'll sell a million copies, and the minute the cat spreads his hand across the neck, you can't give the record away (Brown in Hirshey 1984: 289).

Accounts of Brown's rhythmic orientation are abundant, and generally reiterate the narration of the biographical film, *Soul Connection* (1978), where the commentator remarks that "Brown treated his band like a drum" (Maben [dir.] 1978):

> Brown would sing a semi-improvised, loosely organized melody that wandered, while the band riffed rhythmically on a single chord, the horns tersely punctuating Brown's declamatory phrases. With no chord changes and precious little melodic variety to sustain listener interest, rhythm became everything. Brown and his musicians and arrangers began to treat every instrument and voice in the group as if each were a drum (Palmer in Brackett 1995: 144).

This polyrhythmic integration of Brown's bands stressed the coherence of the ensemble, rather than emphasizing individual virtuosity. While Brown hardly neglected to showcase the abilities of his musicians – indeed his calls to his long-serving saxophonist, Maceo Parker often constituted a major compositional element in itself – the solos were generally contained and always subordinate to the maintenance of rhythmic unity of the ensemble. Moreover, solos were almost always under Brown's strict command as the musicians were directed into keeping the groove together. Brown's troupes for the most part were very much treated like the hired hands that he perceived them to be, and they were, for the most part, denied the individual notoriety enjoyed by the notable jazz counterparts of which they were so enamoured.

Their collective goal was to reinforce repetition as the most expedient way to establish territory. Repetition demands attention perhaps because we attempt to differentiate each instance of it, even if unconsciously. While an often frustrating exercise, repetitious music can hook us in, and thus makes a more expedient claim on territory than that of a more melodically complex music. This is perhaps why we are subjected to repetitive techno being blared from cars, rather than bursts of chamber music. The impact of the beat maintains its consistency over time and space rather than breaking up in the audience's presence. Given the immanent political situation, Brown's musical response was crucial to circumventing the movement-image conventions of previous musical forms, such as jazz for example, musics that were perhaps not as suited to the task of maintaining the required territorial productivity. Brown devised a music would have to make up territory fast, to compensate its audiences for the lost ground that was occurring socially.

Funk thus begins to shape up as an exemplary apprehension of a minor temporality, and reinforcing its "minor" status is an egalitarian nature that allowed for quick circuits of dialogic exchange. Brown's prodigious output, up to eight albums a year, enabled him to maintain an intimate and ongoing dialogue with his audience, which Brown always made sure to address. These dialogues can be heard on his great sixties live albums, such as the *Live at the Apollo* series, where musical numbers often culminated in playful in-jokes with the group that surely must have left large sections of the record-buying public scratching their heads at the time. Furthermore his down-home tributes such as 'There Was a Time' (1967) solidified the esoteric dialogue that Brown maintained with black audiences. Fundamentally a one-chord vamp, the song enticed the audience to think about life down south, replete with call and response where the audience would chant in unison with Brown's cajoling lyric, ". . . the name of the place was Augusta GA." These were songs in dialogue with the diaspora from the South, migrating to the larger cities, taking jobs in the booming industrial North.

Funk's 'Industrial' Elements

In fact, the impact of industry informs funk's clockwork exactitude. While the groove of Brown's music has been attributed to historical African musical practice, I argue, instead, that the tightness and exactitude of James Brown's music owes more to the imminent industrial environment from which it emerged. Brown's musical sensibility of clockwork efficiency conjures up the employment conditions of factories of the North, of its manual labour and piecemeal work developed around the demands of the Taylorism it employed. Brown was no stranger to the ardours of manual labour and he treated his musicians as workers in a funk factory. The industrial influences on the funk groove is further borne out in comments made by Clyde Stubblefield, who has attributed the industrial environmental to the exactitude of his drumming:

> Where I was raised up in Chattanooga TN . . . We had wind up clocks. And they go "tick-tock . . ." all through the whole night. Pitch black dark . . . nothin', you see nothin' . . . and you just hear that "tick-tock . . ." through the whole night and that's time . . . and I go to sleep by that. And then to wake up to a factory, that made wooden cases and they had a chimney that would go . . . shoot puffs of smoke out. We were . . . surrounded by mountains and valley and so when this thing would go "poof" and it would hit the mountains and it would come back and go "poof . . . boom." So that had a rhythm. Washing machine . . . "slish-slosh" . . . that had rhythm. And the train tracks. I was raised up around all those rhythms and I used to walk in time with 'em . . . that's the way it started by me being raised around those types of rhythms (Stubblefield 2003).

In this respect, funk provides a reflection of the industrial experiences of African-American life, with Stubblefield one of its most important aesthetic mediators. In fact, an extrapolation of the extra-machinic and industrial influences that might have impacted on the funk aesthetic have been overlooked. The sense of sheer uncompromising force that could be heard in funk, a music of working-class blacks playing working-class music, is inextricable to its broader conceptual assemblage. In this respect the bigger the band, the mightier the collective force of the music. Each part was a cog in a broader machine, broken down into piecemeal functions. For example, one can only marvel at the intricate guitar figures of Jimmy Nolen, Brown's long-serving guitarist. Nolen's style of playing mostly consisted of minimal percussive patterns, perhaps sharing only half a chord with the second guitarist, or bass player, the horns left to gesture the rest. The parts played by Nolen were often simple, yet incredibly demanding and absolutely unrelenting. One's hand cramps in sympathy with the incessant figures of 'Ain't it Funky Now' (1969) which requires a singular repetitive guitar figure to be played almost continually for the nine minutes of the track's duration.

Brown's funk machine was built from such vital musical cogs, all working together in the constitution of flawless groove. A machine needs spare parts too, and Brown would select from a reserve of musicians which he kept on hand to attempt to replicate any particular sound that he might have in mind. For example, Brown would famously keep a reserve of drummers on hand to translate the aforementioned grunts and groans into a more accessible form of music. As former drummer, Clayton Fillyau, tells Jim Payne, Brown would keep several drummers in reserve: "I've been on shows where we had five drummers and five drum sets set up! And believe me, when you hit that stage, there would be no messing around. All five drummers would be looking at James Brown, 'cause when he pointed his finger at you . . . that next beat, you better be there" (Payne 1996: 29). The musician that most successfully captured his vision would become the player for the track.

This is precisely what happened with the making of the proto-funk single, 'Let Yourself Go' (1966). Recorded fresh after a show at the Latin Casino nightclub, the stripped-down minimalism of the record constitutes a vital episode in the burgeoning funk style. As Brown sings in the track, ". . . it ain't just soul . . . it's just a rhythm and blues." From this time, each successive single would be preoccupied with doing more with less; making use of fewer chords and hitting the groove with ever more ferocity. In the process, Brown became increasingly finicky when it came to replicating the sounds in his head; witness for example the re-released version of 'Let Yourself Go', included on the *Star Time* box set (1991). The newly appended prologue is particularly illuminating. We hear Brown instructing the drummer, John "Jabo" Starks, to hit the snare whenever the singer grunted "uh uh," a process watched from the sidelines by Clyde Stubblefield who was replaced after not being able to deliver during the first couple of run-throughs (G. Brown 1996: 144–45).

That Brown's standards were exacting is an understatement, and he wielded control over his band to the point of tyranny. Brown's ill-will was not only detrimental to the morale of his musicians, but, in the process, brought to a premature close his relationship with some of his best ensembles. In fairness, though, Brown was perhaps the hardest on himself. As the "hardest working man in showbusiness" (Weinger and White 1991: 15) he led by example, and the sheer intensity of Brown's physically and mentally arduous stage show required extraordinary stamina; the pace was so extraordinarily demanding that most musicians would find themselves having to leave eventually, due to burn out: "Everybody would get worn out in that show eventually. Nobody would last over a long period of time" (Stubblefield in Payne 1996: 62). Perhaps the demands Brown placed on himself and the band were his peculiar way of paying respect to his audiences who themselves had to work so hard in often low-paying jobs to afford his shows. Acutely aware that he was singing to the average African-American person, Brown's onstage ritual of being worked to death on stage, looking for the stamina to get up and try again – the essence of his famous cape routine – was a way of playing out the intolerable circumstances of the everyday. Brown was articulating ways of feeling and it is the communal atmosphere that he creates which makes his live albums so enticing.

Given the fact that audiences would soon be delivered back to the capitalist machine, Brown's show had to make the most of time, and the groove's emphasis on the present procured a vital relationship to affective pleasure. The beauty of dancing is, of course, that it is the process of losing one's self in an undetermined form of space/time, outside hegemonically constructed time and space. The necessity of developing events for such becomings gave rise to the block parties and discotheques and would allow the minor cultures to connect with the world again. By connecting, I mean a way of connecting with the world outside of the limitations of imposed time/space, and to do so also required the development of aesthetics that would bring out the possibilities of new relations to time. This is how Brown's music instigated the shift from the "movement-image" conventions of popular music to the types of "time-image" musical conventions inherent to funk, or, more broadly, the foregrounding of affective relations over the action-image idea of narrativized events. While the physicality of dance might appear to be about action and hence related to the action-image, in fact the opposite is true – as understood from an existential point of view. The image of thought behind dancing and its lack of determination of its gestures is the very opposite to the logic of action–reaction and agency.

Minimalism

Brown's funk would emerge at a time of new-found preoccupation with musics that fostered a "time-image" aesthetic, the most prominent of these being the "art" music of "the minimalists." Famous for exponents such as

LaMonte Young, Terry Riley, Philip Glass and Steve Reich, the minimalists were "all . . . to some degree influenced by [John] Cage" (Morgan 1991: 423) and the "understatement rather than exaggeration" of the "oriental influences" behind Cage's work (Morgan 1991: 422). Yet, despite any real declaration of its influence, it would seem inconceivable that the minimalist style could have flourished without being affected by African-American music of the time. Working apart from, but nevertheless concurrently with, the musical embrace of repetition, which drove the minimalist aesthetic, the emergence of funk, and its preoccupation with the temporal, was perhaps not entirely coincidental. That both of these styles would emerge at a similar time in the mid-1960s is surely reflective of a change in musical sensibility to an emphasis on time-image composition that impacted the entire musical landscape.

While Reich, for example, would later discuss the influence of Ghanaian music on his work, it is odd that the music the minimalist composers grew up with, a popular music soundscape dominated by Afro-American derived musical styles, is not given greater credence in the accounts of their compositions. For example, two of Reich's earliest and most well-known works, 'It's Gonna Rain' (1965) and 'Come Out' (1966), both make use of recordings of African-American subjects. Reich's 'It's Gonna Rain', composed in January 1965, makes this influence plain by making the central focus of the piece the voice of a black Pentecostal preacher recorded on the streets of San Francisco. The piece singled out a contraction of a broader sermon until the words "it's gonna rain" were looped over and over in what would appear to an exaggerated monument to the repetition of the black church tradition. In 'Come Out', Reich uses the speech of a young man injured in the Harlem Riots of 1964 whose line "to let the bruise blood come out to show them" follows a similar process.

John Law (1997) will infer minimalism with the power of heterogeneity thus alleviated through a lack of a deterministic, teleological goal, "[f]or in the music of minimalism there is no terminus, no end point," he says. Law will go on to draw parallels between this music and with Deleuze and Guattari's concept of a plateau which "is always in the middle, not at the beginning or the end" (Deleuze and Guattari quoted in Law 1997), remarks that are similarly applicable to the music of Brown:

> So it is with the music of minimalism. There are no great Mozartian vistas. No overviews. No resolutions. Minimalism is always in the middle. There is, except in the most straightforward sense, no beginning and no end. Instead there is tension and incompleteness . . . this is a music, yes, of surfaces. Of displacements. Of minimal and endless transformations. Of discomfort. Of continual movements to find some kind of stable place. That never find a stable place. Of continuing incompleteness. Of continuing. Of incompleteness. Yes, I repeat, of tensions (Law 1997).

In the book *Experimental Pop*, the authors Billy Bergman and Richard Horn write that the "endless, hypnotic funk repetitions" in Brown's music, "come as close as you can get to African and minimalist music" (Bergman and Horn 1985: 15). What links these styles is the effect of tension and anticipation central to both musics, and, not least, the repetition that would continue to emphasize an attention to time over movement.

Time: Aion and Chronos

The message of musics such as gospel, funk and minimalism is time, the shift from the extensive spatiality characteristic of the movement-image to the intensive spatiality of the time-image (Rajchman 2000: 130–31). No longer concerned with the regulation of clock time (chronos) this is a form of time that invokes an "intensive spatiality" that counteracts the "extensive space" that was enforced upon the minor. This notion of intensive space takes one beyond thinking of time in terms of the chronological, pulsed *Chronos* to an apprehension of the time of *Aion*, attributed as it is by Deleuze, as the time of becoming that resides outside of chronological measurement.

In the late nineteenth century, composers such as Satie and Debussy did much to divest Western music from its compositional predilection towards the telos. The chronological time of Western music reflected the vast influence of Enlightenment philosophy and its emphasis on progression, and it is not until the recorded music of the twentieth century that white Western compositional sensibility encounters the music of Afro-America, and ultimately delivers it from its teleological apprehensions. Twentieth-century popular music, infused with Afro-American influence, will increasingly emphasize time as present, rather than as projection, a concept that reaches its apotheosis in popular dance music styles borrowed from gospel and the music of the church. For example the Norman Whitfield production, 'Girl You Need a Change of Mind' (1973), featuring Temptations vocalist Eddie Kendricks, is popularly attributed as the first disco record (Brewster and Broughton 1999: 167). Its inspiration, says Whitfield, is the church: "People always ask me about the breakdown. Well, my background is the church. It's not unusual in a church song to have a breakdown like that" (ibid.). Indeed the artists would reinvigorate a process that was a staple of church celebration, as Kendricks attests: "I stood in the studio with the musicians, giving instructions as we were cutting for them to break it down to nothing, then gradually come in one by one and rebuild the fervour of the song" (ibid.). The groove is the gift of the gospel tradition, and it informs a temporal approach to composition that extends across generations of musical production. It is the harnesssing of Aion, the time of becoming, that unites musical styles both sacred and secular and which will eventually crystallize into the electronic dance music forms of the future. The sense of non-chronological time might be the force attributed to the "experience" of a circular music, discussed here by Cynthia Rose:

> It is experience – constantly revealed, re-lived, and re-interpreted in terms of the fresh, contemporary moment. As James Brown's adaptations of gospel music, his own brand of preaching, and the moral admonitions of his music demonstrate, these are not static but dynamic belief and performance traditions. Improvisation and innovation are expected. In *I Got The Word In Me And I Can Sing It, You Know*, his book on the performed art of the African-American sermon, Gerald L Davis makes the point that "however African-American performance and creativity might be observed, the organizing principle of circularity, rather than linearity, is evident . . . it holds a central, core importance in African-American performance." Whether one calls this "roots" or 'the groove," such an "organizing principle" is easily seen on-stage in the acts of Brown, Clinton, Prince or a jazz ensemble. Across the diaspora, listeners may apprehend its heartbeat in recurring musical phrases or in slices of common slang which turn up again and again . . . Even the young rappers and hip-hop breakdancers of the '80s, whose work is founded on the

> Jamesian beat, sense this history behind their art – not to mention Brown's central role as a conduit of that history (Rose 1990: 121–22).

While the preacher might mediate in the unfolding of the gospel song, his approach differs greatly from the Western conductor who tries to limit improvisation, rather than embrace it. Instead of overseeing a faithful rendition, the preacher (and, by extension, Brown's own relationship with his band) presides over a more aleatory process, a wilful harnessing of uncertainty, an excitement borne from the irrational cut that, as we shall see later in the book, will influence practices of the future such as DJing. In fact, the DJ, who might manipulate a record of Brown's voice to punctuate and "cut" the music as a means to strengthen repetition, is really not that far removed from the role of the preacher in the sermon. Brown's voice exhortations have become ubiquitous in this style of music, where a grunt or a well-timed "Good God!" are conveniently inserted into the sampled work to reiterate an affective intensity. In this context, the Brown sample transcends mere significational value; its multifarious nature encompasses recognition, recollection, context and history, including those hard times and horrors that cannot be articulated but only understood.

Traditional musicology is not well disposed to accounting for these types of machinic musical relations, tending instead to recount what music might "mean," and thus subsume musical forms into narrative. David Brackett's discussion of Brown's 1971 single 'Superbad' is a case in point, an analysis that attempts to tell us what a music might mean, but nothing of how it actually works. To evaluate the music made for dancing, in terms of what it represents, is missing the point. As Simon Reynolds enquires in his *Generation Ecstasy* (1999) should there not be a more suitable theoretical framework for the discussion of popular dance music?

> Rave music represents a fundamental break with rock, or at least the dominant English Lit and socialist realist paradigms of rock criticism, which focuses on songs and storytelling. Where rock relates an experience (autobiographical or imaginary), rave *constructs* an experience. Bypassing interpretation, the listener is hurled into a vortex of heightened sensations, abstract emotions, and artificial energies (Reynolds 1999: 9–10).

The *represented* body is simply redundant within this world of bodily intensity. We should, instead, be focusing upon how the body is enabled to think anew through the affective relations it instigates, a process Deleuze refers to as "becomings rather than stories."

James Brown as Political Figure

It is, of course, the "socialist realist paradigms of rock criticism" to which Reynolds refers that have been responsible for the representation of Brown's legacy. This has meant a surfeit of commentary on what Brown was supposed to have represented, rather than the affective relations that he actually inspired. His often ill-informed dalliances with traditional politics have been a consistent feature of such commentary on Brown's life, and have somewhat clouded his true political legacy.

Take, for example, the now oft-cited Boston Garden performance that Brown performed on 5 April 1968, the very day of Martin Luther King's assassination. At the behest of the city fathers, Brown allowed his performance at the Boston Garden to be filmed in the hope that the telecast would distract members of the black community enough to quell any further rioting. As Brown historians Harry Weinger and Cliff White explain, Brown's actions delivered him a new-found political prominence: "Brown stepped to the fore. The day after King's assassination, he was televised in concert at the Boston Garden to calm the rioting. He was flown to Washington, DC to speak on the radio and urge brotherhood. Brown and his wife were also invited to a White House dinner with President Johnson" (Weinger and White 1991: 34).

Suffice to say, this apparent collusion with "the man" would place significant strain on the goodwill that had been extended to Brown by African-American audiences. It also began a recasting of Brown into an "Uncle Tom," a position that was further exacerbated when he personally requested to play for the troops in Vietnam shortly after. Brown's impeding visit was announced, in fact, by congressman, Tom Atkins, during that very same televised Boston concert. Brown's rationale: "I knew that black soldiers were complaining that the USO didn't send enough acts they could identify with, and I wanted to change that" (Maycock 2003: 70). He lamented the fact that they were doing their bit for their country and then were "rewarded" with entertainers such as Bob Hope (Maycock 2003: 68).

Brown's magnanimity was met with disdain by the more radical elements of black politics, and was tantamount to collusion with the government during the very same period that the Black Panthers were setting up neighborhood chapters to defend themselves against the "man" and as Muhammad Ali declared that, ". . . no Vietcong ever called me nigger." In fact it has been intimated that it was coercion by the Panthers which prompted Brown to produce 'Say It Loud! I'm Black and I'm Proud'.

Fellow King recording artist, and Brown associate, Hank Ballard, claimed that the song was written as a direct result of Brown being threatened by sub-machine gun toting Black Panthers (Vincent 1996: 78). In his recent *second* "autobiography," *I Feel Good* (2005), Brown said that he found a hand grenade with his name on it outside his hotel room on the night of this recording, although he was ignorant of the parties involved (Brown and Eliot 2005).

Brown perhaps knew that the black community was up against overwhelming, perhaps impossible, odds. As Nelson George would write in *The Death of Rhythm and Blues* (1988), the quality of life for African-Americans after the riots of Watts (1965), Newark and Detroit (1967) only had the effect of devastating the little infrastructure that black communities had managed to develop up to that point (George 1988: 97–98). Many main streets in black capitals never recuperated and fell into a state of permanent disrepair (George 1988: 98), and, as the 1970s pressed on, the situation was not rectified.

The immediate aftermath is caught in the documentary, *James Brown: Man to Man* (1968), where Brown can be seen ruminating on the plight of African-Americans living in the ghettos of Watts, Washington and Harlem. Brown was undoubtedly aware of the irony of this situation, and, for his part, attempted in his own way to contain the more destructive effects of the civil-rights struggle. Rather problematically, for many members of the black community, Brown decided, somewhat controversially, to become an advocate of "black capitalism," and followed up with an endorsement of Nixon to boot. Perhaps it was a way of entering into the ultimate dialogue with majoritarian culture; either way it didn't help his somewhat shaky standing in the community.

Of course, not everyone can possess the sense of conviction that Brown was gifted with, and this dogged sense of self-sufficiency was flaunted conspicuously via his mini-empire of Lear Jets, James Brown *Golden Platter* restaurants, and radio stations in Augusta and Baltimore. Brown himself hoped that such achievements against the overwhelming odds would demonstrate to African-Americans what could be attained. In fact, as he sang in the song,

'Funky President' (1975), he thought African-Americans, should stick together ". . . and do like the mob." These calls always very much came from a knowingly minor point of view. For instance, when Brown was to sing, 'You Can Have Watergate, But Gimme Some Bucks and I'll be Straight' (1975), during one of his bands, the JB's solo outings, this does not sound like someone who actually believed in integrating with the dominant culture. Brown's protest tracks are indicative of a general nonchalance to traditional politics: "what does it matter as we are not part of your system anyway."

Given the precarious political position that Brown now had to occupy, it would be unfair to simply attribute Brown's famous riot quelling performances on television as a simple collusion with the enemy. Undoubtedly, from the point of view of a "visible" politics, there *are* real problems with these performances. However, there are other aspects to politics. Brown was perhaps naïvely attempting to address the African-American's ultimate enemy, its lack of visibility. At least if Brown was on stage addressing a televised audience he might demonstrate the potential of African-American political power through what he considered a more productive approach to the situation at hand. I do not believe that Brown's TV appearances, nor Vietnam tours, ultimately undermined his minor status; the fact that he would endure as a hero in the Afro-American community long afterwards is testament to this. Brown was committed to the invention of a "people to come," which is not simply achieved through the promotion of "specific political action or by protesting oppression (although such actions do have their own value), but by inducing processes of becoming-other, by undermining stable power relations and thereby activating lines of continuous variation in ways that have previously been restricted and blocked" (Bogue 2005: 114).

Brown's rallying cry of minority expression, *Say It Loud! I'm Black and I'm Proud*, was perhaps an exemplary step in "undermining stable power relations" as it ultimately trumped Brown's ill-informed political pitches and called upon the invention of a people. As Rickey Vincent explains:

> To a generation of frustrated blacks who understood Malcolm X when he called for freedom "by any means necessary," Brown had touched a nerve. He inspired the poets to dream of Black Revolution, to speak of killing whitey (though not his point of view), and to prepare for redemption on this earth, not the next. Brown had entered the movement. He

influenced everyone, from revolutionary poets Umar Ben Hassan and Gil Scott-Heron to balladeers Marvin Gaye and Stevie Wonder (Vincent 1996: 78).

The fact of the matter is that the track was never totally embraced by Brown. Despite the plaudits it has subsequently received, 'Say It Loud! I'm Black and I'm Proud' received only a handful of performances around the time of its release: "He only did that song live maybe three or four times. Five at the most. Then he stopped doing it" (Rowland 2002: 47), says long-time Brown band member Sweet Charles Sherrell. In a recent interview with Matt Rowland in "rare groove" magazine *Wax Poetics*, Sherrell takes up the story in more detail:

> Well, after I heard the words to it, it kind of frightened me, because you know at that time a whole lot of stuff was going on . . . Martin Luther King and all the riots and stuff. We've been playing, performing for all races of people – I've seen them in the crowd, you know. So [I'm thinking], "this is going to hurt him." Because you can't go to a concert and sit there and say, "say it loud, I'm Black and I'm proud" if you're not Black or if you're not Mexican or whatever. You can't do that so you'd feel cheated, you know. That scared me. But James realised it too. Because all of a sudden his crowds started dropping off (Rowland 2002: 47).

'Say it Loud!' was a victim of its own success and, whatever fears lingered in the community, they stopped Brown being played as readily on mainstream radio that he once was. While it was a Top 10 hit on the white pop charts, the single would be his last to reach the upper reaches of the charts for nearly twenty years. With the increasing uncertainty of the times, the single's strident message would appear to have had the effect of eroding Brown's major "crossover" to the white US audience which he had begun courting only a few years earlier. As Jesse Jackson has commented in relation to the song:

> We always felt that because of being black, we was always put down because of it – but James Brown had the youth to know that it's OK to be who you are . . . a lot of the kids had been wearing hair one way but when James Brown came out

with "I'm Black and I'm Proud" you started to see what we call Naturals and that meant showing Black Pride (Peterzell [dir.] 1995).

'Say it Loud! I'm Black and I'm Proud' was, to quote Rickey Vincent, "a turning point in black music" (Vincent 1996: 78) not only because it affirmed present identity, but because it beckoned the emergence of a new collective – a "people to come." Brown's alterity was further escalated by a number of "black power" hits that would emanate from his production stable, tracks such as Hank Ballard's solo, 'How You Gonna Get Respect (When You Haven't Cut Your Process Yet)' (1968) and 'Blackenized' (1969). Albert Goldman once formulated an essay with the equation "Black Power = James Brown" (Goldman 1968/1992).

While much is made of Brown's overtly political narratives such as 'Say it Loud! I'm Black and I'm Proud' (1968) or 'I Don't Want Nobody to Give Me Nothing (Open Up the Door I'll Get it Myself)' (1969) to merely perceive the political message of Brown's music through his lyrics would hardly do the man's political legacy adequate justice. For, as indicated earlier in the chapter, Brown's real political legacy is that his music would provide a belief in the world as an exploration of affective possibility. It was the politics of bodily action found in the tightly integrated music and choreography that made Brown such a presence on stage, such as the aforementioned *T.A.M.I. Show*. It is as this arbiter of bodily affect that kept Brown in stead with later generations, as a purveyor of a music that anticipates the decline in simple sensory-motor driven songs. For Brown's funk, even in its early stages, had already begun to show signs of this shift in existential conditions reflected for instance in Brown's rather ambivalent relationship to the orthodox verse/chorus/verse forms of composition.

In terms of musical currency, Brown's non-political tracks were arguably even more important than his more overt political commentary. Providing the ingredients for later political import through hip-hop and other dance musics are songs that veer between the esoteric to the downright bizarre – titles such as 'Let a Man Come in and Do the Popcorn' (1969), one of the many "Popcorn" related records Brown released in the period of 1968–1969 and designed to cash in on a rather obscure dance craze; 'I Can't Stand Myself (When You Touch Me)' (1968) which is basically a riff repeated for seven minutes; and 'I'm Tired But I'm Clean' (1963), the musical content just as bizarre as the title itself.

The experimentalism inherent in these tracks is just as important as the well-regarded strident narratives of 'Say it Loud! I'm Black and I'm Proud' (1968) or 'I Don't Want Nobody to Give Me Nothing, (Open Up the Door I'll Get it Myself)' (1969). The fact is that part of funk's power lay in its pure abstraction. It was this abstraction that would instigate new thought, as well as new creative practices, both musical as well as social, that came with that thought. Thought without presupposition. For true to the sheer pragmatic function of the Idiot, Brown did not mistakenly assume presuppositions of intent or align his work to some transcendental project that would undermine its very newness. We might recall here the comment made by Brown, that funk was not the result of some preconception or even direction: "*funk was not a project . . . the thing was ahead*" (Brown in Rose 1990: 59).

In general, it is the realm of the macropolitical that tends to be the most commonly accepted method of guaranteeing a political future, yet it is the artist, rather than the State, who can most expediently catalyse imminent affective concerns into a form of collective enunciation. If the teleology that drove the soul aesthetic was collapsing at this time, alongside the failure of the civil-rights trajectory, there is little that the State can do to circumvent the demise of an existential relation to history. Within such disconcerting circumstances, Brown would have to maintain the most important attribute of the artist, the promotion of a belief in the world rather than merely succumbing to its failures:

> The whole relation of thought to action or agency had to change; the problem of "representing the masses" would be rethought in relation to the space and time of minorities in accordance with a new pragmatism, a new empiricism in relation to the world or to trust in the world (Rajchman 2000: 26).

In this respect, I credit Brown with helping to inspire a vital and wholly necessary empiricist conversion, or a belief in the world as imminent possibility, when the bottom fell out of the "transcendent" narratives of soul. For as the social movement underpinning the civil-rights struggle began to collapse, Brown's funk would present one of the more accessible possibilities for establishment of presence in the world. Eschewing the teleology of traditional politics, Brown's extrovert performances were indicative of an awareness that only a belief in the body can provide the means to "become," and that "becoming" is ultimately the only real political possibility for a "minor" people.

5 The Godfather of Post-Soul

The malaise felt by many African-Americans in the 1970s was exacerbated by an increasingly uncertain political trajectory, as the hopes of the 1960s soul generation took a turn for the worse. With the assassination of King in 1968, and the decline in the optimism of the civil-rights era that subsequently transpired from this event, we witness an accompanying break in soul's "action-image." Compounded by the political casualties of the preceding decade, including the assassinations of Medger Evers and Malcolm X, as well as the systematic prosecution of the Black Panthers and other political movements, the lack of belief in progression led to an overall decline in political ideology, a situation which, in turn, would affect the music that was being made. As Atlantic Records' Jerry Wexler comments in the documentary, *The Soul of Stax* (1994), "What had been the soul era, on the high road, suddenly, seemed to grind to a shuddering halt. There was frustration, there was rage – but worst of all – the spirit seemed to have gone out of this particular movement of rhythm and blues music" (Wexler in Priestley [dir.] 1994). If soul began to lose momentum, it took with it the market for soul music, which, as Gerri Hirshey asserts, "seemed to have reached its peak in 1968, when Billboard reported, R&B DISKS SWING TO 'BLACK HOPE.' Within a year it would declare, BACKLASH CUTS SOUL ON TOP 40" (Hirshey 1985: 315).

The Post-Soul Era

This decline of the existential narratives driving soul's "image of thought" impels an existential disarray referred to, perhaps not surprisingly, as the beginning of the "post-soul" era. It was writer Nelson George who coined the term "post-soul," in reference to an African-American population trying to come to terms with life in the aftermath of the civil-rights struggle. Studies of this "post-soul generation" have, in turn, been the subject of George's books including *Buppies, B-boys, Baps and Bohos: Notes on Post-Soul Black Culture* (1992) and the recent *Post-Soul Nation* (2004). An academic embellishment of George's concept appeared in Mark Anthony Neal's *Soul Babies: Black Popular Culture and the Post-Soul Aesthetic* (2002), where he uses the term post-soul to "describe the political, social and cultural experiences of the African-American community since the end of the civil rights and Black Power movements" (Neal 2002: 63). While the term "post-soul" was initially coined by George as a general description of "black popular culture after the blaxploitation era" (Neal 2002: 63), Neal will instead place more emphasis on locating a "post-soul generation" around a more refined set of events, namely:

> folks born between the 1963 March on Washington and the [*Regents of the University of California v. Bakke* challenge to affirmative action in 1978], children of soul, if you will, who came to maturity in the age of Reaganomics and experienced the change from urban industrialism to deindustrialism, from segregation to desegregation, from essential notions of blackness to metanarratives on blackness, without any nostalgic allegiance to the past (back in the days of Harlem, or the thirteenth-century motherland, for that matter), but firmly in grasp of the existential concerns of this brave new world (Neal 2002: 3).

Neal outlines the emergence of this post-soul sensibility through specific examples to be found in the music, film and television of this post-civil-rights generation. His analysis takes in such texts as the work of R&B singer R. Kelly, Melvin Van Peebles' *Sweet Sweetback's Baadasssss Song*, African-American centred sitcoms and TV shows of the 1960s–1980s, and the "post-soul intelligentsia" of the 1980s – a group of artists and writers such as Greg Tate, Vernon Reid, the Black Rock Coalition, Jean-Michel Basquiat, George C. Wolfe, Darius James, Cassandra Wilson and Geri Allen – to name but a few examples (Neal 2002). A key "post-soul" text of this period, according to Neal, is the television sitcom, *Good Times*, which revolves around the trials and tribulations of the Chicago-based Evans family whose acute existential disarray epitomized the lives of many African-American families trying to cope in a post-civil-rights period.

The existential disarray exacerbated by this crisis in "movement" – or the decline in the belief of action-image and its teleological revelation of "truth" – presents further conceptual parallels with the shift from action-image to time-image discussed in Deleuze's *Cinema* books. The decline in soul's "action-image" is exacerbated by circumstances similar to those that drove the breakdown of the movement-image aesthetic: "an image of Truth as globalizing or totalizing apperception, linking humanity and the world as commensurable points in a sensorimotor whole . . . in an indirect image of time" (Rodowick 1997: 184). That is to say, soul's "action-image" was about instigating movement in a hegemonic conception of time and history, and a belief in truth as a product of this relationship. Thus the break in the action-image exacerbated through post-soul malaise reflects "that the ideal of the true was the most profound fiction" (Deleuze 1989: 149) and from where a pondering of this breakdown in linear time, rendered aesthetic, might propose a new-found relationship with the powers of the false, as "[m]aking-false becomes the sign of a new realism, in opposition to the making-true of the old" (Deleuze 1986: 213).

As we shall see in this chapter, it is the "powers of the false," such as the repurposed Brown samples, which reflect this re-evaluation of truth. According to Deleuze, it is Nietzsche's "will to power" that "substitutes the power of the false for the form of the true, and resolves the crisis of truth, wanting to settle it once and for all, but, in opposition to Leibniz, in favour of the false and its artistic, creative power" (Deleuze 1989: 131). This "creative power" has particular utility for the post-soul era, whereby, in the absence of truth, we get instead a new regime of falsity, or as Neal attributes to the post-soul aesthetic, the "bastardization" central to its aesthetic. Marked by its cynicism towards the determinism of the preceding soul generation, the emergent "post-soul aesthetic" will "willingly 'bastardize' black history and culture to create alternative meanings, a process that was largely introduced to the post-soul generation via the blaxploitation films of the 1970s" (Neal 2002: 22).

Bastardization

As it is constitutive of the post-soul aesthetic, we might accommodate this concept of "bastardization" as a practice inherently concerned with the drawing out of the co-existent temporal alterity that resides in the official representation of history. In the examples that we will attend to in this chapter, the death of the action-image's will to a teleological truth will create the conditions for the production of a music that invokes an "irrational" relationship to time. Thus, one of the most salient examples of an aesthetic manifestation of this "irrational" relationship to time is the music of the DJs who, in the process of cutting up old records in search of a groove, will render visible the many possible futures that reside virtually in these musical refrains. Bolstered by new capacities for manipulation presented by digital technology, we are presented with a burgeoning sampling culture that will reassemble these "sheets of past" into new temporal assemblages. The message of such compositions of time is that a new future is always virtually contained in the present, waiting to be unlocked. Of course there needs to be a catalyst for this new enterprise to emerge, and what drives this creative experimentation is an accompanying "shock to thought" (Deleuze 1989: 156). As it might be conceived in terms of the post-soul aesthetic, this "shock to thought" is a reaction to the "intolerable" decline of the preceding soul aesthetic.

These trying existential circumstances beckon a creative reaction that might overturn its conditions, and provide the means to rethink the world, in turn. Brown's own reaction to intolerable conditions was the creation of funk, an aesthetic which promoted affect and a force for becoming, a belief in *this* world and of the present, rather than one of teleological projection. For the samplers and DJs of the post-soul experience, this force for becoming was activated in the re-appropriation of Brown's music (among many others) for affectively driven connection. For Deleuze, a belief in *the* world is the means by which we can remain open to the potential connections that might be discovered when one relinquishes a more dogmatic conception of the world.

To return to his cinematic example, the catalyst for the shift from the movement to time-image aesthetic was the atrocities of World War II, evidence indeed that "common sense" does not always result in progress. These intolerable results of the war drove the crisis in this adherence to the logic of action-image where "the link between man and the world is broken" (Deleuze 1989: 171–72). In terms of Deleuze's cinematic example, the crisis in the action-image is reflected materially in subsequent periods of European cinema, including the Italian neo-realist cinema of the late 1940s, the French Nouvelle Vague of the late 1950s and 1960s, and the new West German cinema roughly a decade later (Deleuze in Flaxman 2000: 34). That these cinematic periods were working through their own particular existential crises can be evidenced in the new methods sought to depict time and space differently in their respective oeuvres.

In this chapter, we look to Brown's role as catalyst in the construction of a musical time-image, one that might strengthen affective connection and overcome the "intolerable" circumstances of the post-soul era. For the musics of the post-soul era owe much to Brown's pioneering of the groove-oriented funk style, expressed not only through funk, but through disco and beyond. In the late 1960s and early 1970s, Brown's groove indicated a way out of soul's predilection for projection and, in the process, impels Afro-America's pre-eminent music genre of that decade.

Evolution of the Groove

To gauge the effect Brown had on the transformation of black music in the 1960s, one only has to look to Brown's *Live at the Apollo* series of albums – the original *Live at the Apollo* (1963) to *Live at the Apollo 2* (1968) and finally *Revolution of the Mind: Live at the Apollo 3* (1971). Each album signposted a radical shift in Brown's musical sensibility. For instance, the original *Live at the Apollo* album saw Brown maintaining a fairly orthodox style of composition although a taste of things to come can be witnessed in the extended vamping of 'Lost Someone', generally pleading over lost love, and singing songs that wouldn't have sounded out of place in any contemporary soul revue. By contrast, *Live at the Apollo 2*, recorded less than five years later, marked the beginning of the extraordinary one-chord jam workouts more characteristic of Brown's funk style, witnessed for example in the twenty-plus-minute tour de force medley of 'There Was a Time/I Feel All Right/Cold Sweat'. By 1971's *Live at the Apollo 3*, the funk groove was the rule, with only the odd, brief flashback to his late 1950s–early 1960s soul canon. The third instalment of the *Apollo* series was also more audacious in its politics, and Brown is on record deliberately conversing with his musicians on "black consciousness," vocalizing his satisfaction with the symbolic value of Fred Wesley's black trombone. The *Live at the Apollo 3* album was completely removed from its original predecessors not only in terms of composition, but also in regards to general existential outlook; there was no chance that Brown could have launched into jokes about the Ku Klux Klan back in 1962 as he does on the latter album. Thus one must only compare the stylistic development that Brown made between these albums to see how the new musical regime would instead reflect a new expression/experience of time, "rather than motion" (Deleuze 1995: 59).

Thus funk provides the creative conditions for which the music of the post-soul generation could subsequently build upon, where Brown's music indicates an attempt to apprehend an alternate sense of time and space that might be seen to exist outside the telos, an alternative to the decline of narrative that was the overriding existential condition of the social. When

Brown put his faith in the groove, he put his faith in the specific and immediate interaction of bodies and the becoming that would transpire from them. For this reason, Brown's music is entirely pragmatic in the sense that it brings bodies together in new ways, all the while affirming the possibility of a belief in probabilistic futures that begin *now* – even if the broader message of the macropolitical world was somewhat less than affirmative. The becomings to transpire from the creative potential of dance and bodily movement were courted by the long, unrelenting and intricate grooves that Brown pioneered.

It is perhaps no coincidence that Brown's emphasis on groove took hold around the very time that the sequential, chronological action–reaction of the soul narratives were in disarray. In fact, it was post-1968 that Brown's tracks took on an increasingly minimalist aesthetic, as indicated by tracks such as 'Ain't It Funky Now' (1969) or 'Give It Up or Turnit a Loose' (1969). These tracks were increasingly stripped down, even compared to the titles that had appeared a few years prior. Melodic structure was dispensed with, and the tracks would increasingly rely on a single chord sustained ad infinitum, with perhaps only the briefest of bridges to "cut" the groove and strengthen the anticipation within the track.

This emergence of a rhythmically driven groove might also be constitutive of an alternate form of temporality, the time of Aion, which instead of measuring the sequential "motion" of chronos, is concerned instead with the time of becoming – a becoming that is not to be found through political movement but instead through the affective possibilities of the groove. By way of harnessing this non-linear approach to compositional time, DJs and the sampling cultures would strip the "breakbeats" from old soul records and reassemble them in a new and ambiguous fashion. The styles to emerge from this post-soul era, manifest in genres from hip-hop to disco, techno and house, will all, in some way, eschew sequential composition to instead take up a musical montage based on irrational cuts and the non-chronological assembly of pre-recorded material.

This music might be seen to have been more open to an engagement of a more "probabilistic" rather than "deterministic" universe. As D. N. Rodowick explains, the shift from movement-image to time-image indicates a

> change in the order of sense [which] implies change in the nature of belief. The organic regime believes in identity,

unity, and totality. It describes a deterministic universe where events are linked in a chronological continuum: one believes retroactively in a past that leads inevitably to the present; one has faith in a future that emerges rather predictably out of the present ... Alternatively, the regime of the time-image replaces this deterministic universe with a probabilistic one (Rodowick 1997: 15).

The groove is, of course, anything but deterministic – that's how one gets lost in it.

Tougher Grooves for Tougher Times

The circularity of Brown's grooves undermined the telos of hegemonic time. Not only would this reconstitution of time distinguish funk from the compositional methods that had characterized soul, which were relatively orthodox from a compositional point of view, but it would ensure Brown's ongoing regard as an affirmative force amid post-soul existential malaise; a force for becoming, where few continued to exist. Even by the late 1970s when Brown's commercial cache had waned somewhat, his work would remain vital to the DJs of the block parties, as Afrika Bambaataa explains:

> [Record companies] were just shoving disco down our throats. For the first two years, we were playing it, and that was cool. But the dancers in the black and Latino community change every three months. Then after the third and fourth year, they were trying to get rid of the funk. You weren't hearing James [Brown] and Sly [and the Family Stone] on the radio much, so to keep the audiences kicking with the funk, we started adding all their stuff, and other funky beats, to our musical repertoire (Bambaataa in Reighley 2000: 45).

For these DJs respected the inordinate influence that Brown had on facilitating the groove so essential to their own musically driven becoming. A music that would, of course, be further extrapolated by other funk and disco groups throughout the 1970s, groups such as the Ohio Players, Kool and the Gang, the Meters and of course Parliament-Funkadelic – George Clinton's patented brand of "P-Funk." In distinction to the James Brown of the 1960s and 1970s (but not the 1980s) who was vehemently opposed to drugs, Clinton was anything but. Clinton's Parliament-Funkadelic was literally a James Brown band on acid, as his active recruitment of disgruntled ex-Brown musicians from the early 1970s bolstered his funk supergroups. Initially taking in dissidents of the original JBs, including Bootsy and Catfish Collins and Frank Waddy, Brown's despotic sensibility affected a consistent exodus into the mid-1970s, resulting in the recruitment of former James Brown alumni such as Fred Wesley and Maceo Parker, in turn. For this reason, Parliament-Funkadelic is perhaps the closest bridge between Brown and the burgeoning post-Brown funk styles, including disco, that would accompany Brown throughout the 1970s.

The repetitive grooves of the funk style featured heavily in the soundtrack of the post-soul generation, as its grooves beckoned the affective power of dance. It is not surprising, then, that all of the pioneering DJs, for example, Francis Grasso in disco, and Kool Herc, Afrika Bambaataa and Grandmaster Flash – the last three, hip-hop's pioneering triumvirate – were initially dancers (Brewster and Broughton 2000: 145; KRS-One in Batey 2002: 59; Ogg and Upshal 1999: 15, 37), and it was through dance that Brown's influence was always keenly felt. His appearance on TV shows such as *Shindig* and *The Ed Sullivan Show* in the 1960s and *Soul Train* in the 1970s enabled his communication of the latest dance trends, some of which Brown himself was responsible for creating, including his own "James Brown." While the intense athleticism of his choreographed moves were not unprecedented (the Nicholas Brothers, for example, had been there long before), Brown differed from the athletic dancers that had preceded him if only because he managed to direct a band at the same time. Turning the beat on a dime, Brown would transition between songs, maintaining the twirls, splits and the lightning-fast combinations of his dance routines, all the while feeding this intensity back into the music.

Brown's latest dance steps were something that many African-Americans kids, in particular, had been engaged with since the schoolyard. For instance, Public Enemy's Chuck D reminisces about dancing on ice in the school grounds "During the slippin' and slidin' a few of us had to turn it into the customary challenge, 'try this move and swing like JAMES BROWN.' To do the JAMES BROWN you had to start off with 'I Feel Good, Duh-DUH-dah dah dudda dat'" (Chuck D 1998).

Brown's music was a means of becoming for many black children, and it is a gauge of Brown's iconic status that his name was invoked in everyday activities such as adolescent skipping games:

> I went downtown
> To see James Brown.
> He gave me a nickel
> To buy a pickle.
> The pickle was sour.
> He gave me a flower.
> The flower was dead,
> So this is what he said:
> Hopping on one foot, one foot, one foot.
> Hopping on two foot, two foot, two foot.
> Hopping on three foot . . .
> Hopping on four foot . . . (Riddell cited in Gaunt 2004: 255).

That Brown's music was so profoundly inculcated into the lives of African-American kids would necessarily sustain his influence in the hearts of the post-soul generation for years to come. As Gaunt explains, "Brown is the epitome of coordinating movement with a range of vocal expression, rhymes and speech about movement" (Gaunt 2004: 256). Yet the general effect of this "movement" translated somewhat differently in an existential sense. It was this more "irrational" negotiation of time and space that energized his dance routines, the necessary affordances for these dances constitutive of the composition itself. Brown's pioneering dance moves were thus imperative in his approach to making music and his records contained the necessary stops, starts and gaps of anticipation that would maintain the groove so effectively. The holistic nature of this multi-modal experience, and the intensity it provided, ensured the prominence of Brown's music in the DJ sets:

> In manifold ways, hip-hop is his child. No 1, Brown's beats provide much of the whole art's foundation. Before sampling made it possible to repossess Maceo's soulful squeal, Jabo's different strokes or JB's personal shrieks, when the whole hiphop experience was still live on club turntables or hot-wired out of lamps in the parks and streets (early, free electric sources) b-boys would scour New York in search of old

Brown 45s. Stuck onto larger vinyl – for better mixing grip – these copies of 'Sex Machine,' 'Funky Drummer' or 'Get Up, Get Into It and Get Involved' would be mixed with sounds as diverse as The Incredible Bongo Band's version of 'Apache' or Grand Central Station's 'the Jam' (Rose 1990: 147).

This "irrational" approach to composing or remixing was arrived at through an attendance to the intensity of the groove. As Kool Herc attests: "Breakdancing started with James Brown. He was the king, A-1, B-boy, way back in '69! People started going off, dancing like that to particular records because they had a hype to them. I tagged the name of B-boy to the dancers. I used to call them 'break boys'" (Herc in Batey 2002: 59). Then-contemporary Brown singles such as 'Give it Up or Turnit a Loose' were seminal influences on earlier breakbeat culture (Fernando Jr 1999: 15), and the breakdancers would respond to Brown's grooves with the intensity they deserved. Of particular significance to this burgeoning culture was Brown's 1972 recording, 'Get On the Good Foot' (1972), a record which played a seminal role in the birth of breaking, as discussed here by Crazy Legs from the Rock Steady Crew:

> It's like Bambaataa says, it's an extension of "the Good Foot." When James Brown put that record out, brothers would dance to it and add other moves to it. People would say, "Oh, he's goin' off!" So, they would call it "goin' off." Or they would call it "the boi-oi-oing." Eventually Kool Herc labeled it "B-Boying." He would say, "B-Boys, are you ready?" And that would signify that the break beat was coming on, so break boys and break girls, everybody knew to tie up your laces (Legs in Lascaibar 1998: 27).

As the breakdance movement spearheaded the global hip-hop movement, Brown maintained a central role in proceedings, as reiterated here by UK DJ Tim Westwood: "We were playing Brown for the dancers, the breakers and the bodypoppers – from the very earliest, streetstyle British jams. Stuff like 'Get on the Good Foot'; breakdancing used to be called 'goodfoot', after that record" (Rose 1990: 149). "Breaking" or "breakdancing" was thus named for the fact that the dances were based around the record's "break." The "break" – short for breakbeat – refers to a short section of a record where the other instruments are stripped from the sonic picture, leaving the rhythm section to maintain the groove unaccompanied.

It was perhaps the "irrational" nature of a music constructed through extending disconnected breaks that inspired a form of dancing just as irrational to accompany it. By leaving its reiteration to the whim of the DJ, the breakdancers had no idea when that particular section of the record would stop, and the inherent uncertainty of this situation had the effect of cranking up the intensity level. This uncertainty of the irrational cut takes precedence over the certainty of the straight playback of a record that proposes a more navigable linear trajectory. Again, Brown had already anticipated this by making uncertainty and anticipation part of his musical oeuvre – "When will he take the band to the bridge?"

In his funk records of the late 1960s, from 'Cold Sweat' onwards, Brown gave the breakbeat a new prominence, embracing as he did an increasingly deconstructive (and reconstructive) approach to the music – stripping it down and building it back up – a revelation of the mechanics of his funk machine. While Brown did not invent the breakbeat, it had been a feature of jazz, for example, for many years prior; it was no longer a simple musical diversion, but became an inherent part of the compositional process. As Chris Sharp remarks in *Modulations* (2000): "However you want to define it, the logic of the breakbeat is hip-hop's gift to the world and the most crucial development in popular music since James Brown almost invented the 'give the drummer some' interlude with 'Cold Sweat' in 1967" (Sharp 2000: 153).

As Brown had staggered upon the affective intensity of the breakbeat, he made sure to exploit it for its power. As testimony to this, we have one of Brown's most famous dialogues on record, his instruction to drummer Clyde Stubblefield before the "break" on 'Funky Drummer' (1970): "don't do no soloing brother / just keep what you got / don't turn it loose / cause it's a mother." In other words, a solo will only dilute the intensity of the groove. When Brown strips the music down to its essence in the "engine room" of the rhythm section, it is like he is experimenting with the power of the groove, to simplify the elements just before the point of complete breakdown. A wide-eyed rhythmic scientist pulling apart the groove to see how it ticks, and experimenting with the capacity of the beat's expedient method of territorial creation, to deliver to a people that lacked it.

Brown's new proclivity to harness the power of the break, would, in the process, create "affordances" that would be subsequently capitalized upon in a creative evolution of DJing and sampling culture – in particular, the way that funk opened up compositional practice and the expression of duration in new ways. If soul's "movement-image" was generally based on the more orthodox, sequential forms of composition then out of the post-soul era emerged a new form of music that was based around a more serially constituted groove, one that was constituted through the bastardization of old records by DJs who reconfigured breaks to extend time through irrational cuts and linkages. The "movement-image" recordings subjected to this practice were given over to a new time-image existence, as the records that carried the former narratives of soul were cut up and rearranged into a new non-linear assemblage. By eliminating the conventional song structure, DJs can capitalize on this most "affective" part of the track. As David Toop has explained: "This appropriated music was then edited on record turntables in real time, in order to eliminate the verse, chorus, verse, bridge structure of popular song, leaving only repetitions of an internally complex percussive cell, a fragment and memory trace of the history of a track known as the break" (Toop 2000: 92).

DJs would dispense with the artifice and hone in on the most affective part of the record exorcizing the parts of the song rendered redundant by the audience's dancing needs: "Why do we have to put up with the artifice of structure and melodic ornamentation when we are really looking forward to the most affective part of the song – breakbeat?" or as Method Man, member of hip-hop collective Wu-Tang Clan, once asked in the track 'Method Man' (1993), "How many licks does it take to get to the Tootsie Roll centre of a break?" The intensity of the break fosters the relationship with Aion, the time of becoming, newly extricated from the chronos of the record's duration. For this reason, the aesthetic practices behind electronic dance music genres might reflect a more intensive relationship to time rather than to sequentially based compositional movement. These styles of music make the transition from movement-image to time-image, where the latter will instead attempt to build on the indeterminate repetition of the groove for a more immersive dance experience. For such electronic dance musics work on the premise that their audience will become "lost" in such repetitive grooves rather than concern themselves with following the more linear trajectory of the more orthodox pop tune. As Jamaican-born hip-hop pioneer, Kool Herc, explains:

> I used to hear the gripes from the audience on the dance floor. Even myself, 'cause I used to be a breaker (breakdancer). Why didn't the guy let the record play out? Or why cut it off there? So with that, me gathering all this information around me, I say: "I think I could do that." So I started playing from a dance floor perspective. I always kept up the attitude that I'm not playing it for myself, I'm playing for the people out there (Herc in Ogg and Upshal 1999: 13).

Outside of Francis Grasso's work in the discothèques, Herc was one of the first to recognize the aesthetic potential of the break. He would, for example, take the re-recorded version of 'Give it Up or Turnit a Loose' found on Brown's 1970 album *Sex Machine* (1970) and break it up and "reassemble it" according to his own logic (Fernando Jr 1999: 15). The album version of 'Give it Up or Turnit a Loose' featured the more predominant Clyde Stubblefield break and ". . . Herc noticed that when he played, for example, James Brown's 'Give It Up or Turnit A Loose,' people went especially wild during the 'break' segment of the song, when just the drums or percussion took over" (Fernando Jr 1999: 15). Herc decided to extend this break section in order to embrace "the moment" which was then extended as long as possible through repetition. The practice had emerged from the days when the DJs took a 45rpm record that they would stick onto LPs for better manipulation of the break (Rose 1990: 147):

> Herc wondered what would happen if he got two copies of the same record and cut back and forth between them in order to prolong the break or sonic climax. Unwittingly, Herc had stumbled upon the breakbeat, the starting point for much hip hop, dance, techno, and jungle (drum 'n' bass) today (Fernando Jr 1999: 15).

Given Herc's Caribbean pedigree, and the sound system he used to publicly broadcast his musical experiments, hip-hop has been cited as the great marriage of Afro-Caribbean and African-American cultures (Szwed 1999: 8–9), yet it is not often pointed out that Brown played a seminal role in this nexus. When DJ Kool Herc's reggae records failed to gain traction with Bronx youth, the hip-hop pioneer turned his attention to Brown's records instead: "In his early parties Herc even played Reggae and dub, although, he says, 'I never had the audience for it. People wasn't feelin' reggae at the time. I played a few but it wasn't catching'" (Brewster and Broughton 2000: 229). A burgeoning hip-hop culture was thus built upon the funk and Latin music his Bronx audiences were already used to: "I'm in Rome, I got to do what the Romans do. I'm here. I got to get with the groove that's here" (ibid.). Herc's revised set-list included liberal helpings of Brown's beats including tracks such as the aforementioned 'Give it Up or Turnit a Loose' (1970) (ibid.).

A long-term James Brown fan, Herc had been listening to his records since a child in Jamaica, and prior to his subsequent emigration to the US in 1967: ". . . his mom, who was living in New York, regularly sent him the latest James Brown and Motown 45s" (George 1999: 16). In fact, Brown's influence on the music of the Caribbean has also not received as much attention as it deserves, given the evidence of his influence on local producers. For example, in the March 2002 edition of music magazine, *Mojo*, legendary producer, Lee "Scratch" Perry, cited Brown as his major influence:

> From when I started in the music business in Kingston . . . it was James Brown that inspire me . . . James Brown was the best showman. Everything that man did was to put on a show for the people . . . He take trouble to make sure everything perfect every time . . . Everything going into that show. It what the people want, and I wanted to put on a show like that (Perry and Bradley 2002: 61).

Perry is well known as one of the pioneers of the relatively avant-garde-sounding "dub" which subjected previously recorded tracks to a liberal coating of effects such as reverb and echo as a way of creating new "versions" of these recordings. This process of versioning, a nascent form of the remix, practised by Perry alongside other dub pioneers such as King Tubby, may also have been influenced by Brown. In Lloyd Bradley's superlative *Bass Culture* (2001), he writes that this practice of creating new instrumental versions may have been influenced by Brown's practice of putting an instrumental "Part 2" on the B-sides of his singles (Bradley 2001: 313). Brown made use of multipart singles as he was unable to be contained by the limitations of the 7-inch single. Instead he began to use both A and B sides for tracks, split into "Parts 1 and 2," and when that wasn't enough, used further singles to complete the track. For example, 1971's 'Make It Funky' was initially released on one single with "Parts 1 and 2" covering A and B-side and with "Part 3" (another section of the same track) on the next single. This type of staggered release was also used for two separate single releases to come from the 1973 remake of 'Think'. As Cynthia Rose has commented, Brown's idiosyncratic use of 7-inch singles would foreshadow later innovations such as the 12-inch of the disco period (Rose 1990: 103). As Cynthia Rose writes, "What Brown's circular, extended vamps really needed was that 12-inch single format brought to prominence by disco (and dominant throughout the '80s via soul hits, rap releases and club remixes)" (Rose 1990: 103). Brown's groove-based funk tore away from the more conventional and linear compositional structures of R&B and would result in that music's gradual displacement by the more groove-oriented genres such as funk and disco:

> As the blueprint of a repetitiveness operating on the borderline of monotony, the nearly nine minute-long pieces like 'Hot Pants' or 'Sex Machine' are direct predecessors of the dance remixes that would only be invented for disco years later. In addition, the groundwork was laid for the idea of the remix, in Brown's recording of songs in two parts, the second part usually being an instrumental version, the idea of a variation (Poschardt 1998: 117).

The non-linear, serial repetition of rhythms, which were so important to Brown's oeuvre, beckoned an immersion borne of an alleviation from linear structure. This form of "irrational" composition was not only at the heart of break culture, but was similarly, and concurrently, utilized in the music of disco, which pursued a similar extension of breaks:

> In disco the musical pulse is freed from the claustrophobic interiors of the blues and the tight scaffolding of R&B and early soul music. A looser, explicitly polyrhythmic attack pushes the blues, gospel and soul heritage into an apparently endless cycle where there is no beginning or end, just an ever-present "now." Disco music does not come to a halt . . . restricted to a three-minute single, the music would be rendered senseless. The power of disco lay in saturating dancers

and the dance floor in the continual explosion of its presence (Chambers in Werner 2000: 207).

The Medium of a New Duration

It is in service of disco's invocation of the ever-present "now" that the 12-inch record emerged as the material expression of these new forms of composition, a direct consequence of this increased emphasis on temporal immersion. As Brewster and Broughton recount in their book, the first 12-inch single, 'So Much For Love' by Moment of Truth, was made by Tom Moulton, "for a very select group of his DJ friends and although Roulette later released it on 7-inch, the larger format was never commercially available" (Brewster and Broughton 1999: 170).

The 12-inch format was the culmination of several years of experiments in groove taking place in the late 1960s–early 1970s in discothèques by DJ/producers such as Francis Grasso, Walter Gibbons and Tom Moulton, all of whom would experiment with a burgeoning remix culture intended to make their favourite tracks, "longer and more danceable" (Brewster and Broughton 1999: 167). Moulton was one of the first people to gain notoriety for remixing, credited with remixing cuts as early as 1972 (Brewster and Broughton 1999: 167). Moulton had "the idea of producing a tape specifically made for dancing" (Brewster and Broughton 1999: 167) and remarked that he "thought it was a shame that the records weren't longer, so people could really start getting off" (Moulton in Brewster and Broughton 1999: 167). Brewster and Broughton discuss how Moulton's "forays into editing soon led him to studio-based remixing" (Brewster and Broughton 1999: 168) giving BT Express an R&B No.1 single with his re-edit to 'Do It 'Till You're Satisfied' in mid-1974 (Brewster and Broughton 1999: 168).

While the culmination in the invention of the 12-inch single was just as much accident as anything else, as the story goes, Moulton, having run out of 7-inch blanks, took up the offer of the mastering engineer to press the track on 12-inch (Brewster and Broughton 1999: 170). While the first 12-inch singles were limited to test pressings made by Moulton of his mixes, "[e]ventually, though, the record companies got wise to the benefits of the 12-inch and started using the format for DJ-only promotion. No one is exactly sure when these label-sanctioned promotional 12-inches arrived on the streets, though the general view is that the first was *Dance Dance Dance* by Calhoun, in spring 1975" (Brewster and Broughton 1999: 170).

An interesting but little discussed fact is that the father of the disco remix, Tom Moulton, began his career in the early 1960s as a promotions man at James Brown's recording home, King Records (Moulton, Brewster and Broughton 1998). While the aesthetic manifestation of this relationship can only be speculative, it is a no less than uncanny connection. As Brown was King's biggest artist, it is perhaps interesting to consider just how Brown's music influenced Moulton in creeping up the length of the records. There is also the fact that Brown had had some experience putting together re-edits himself at King. In 1969, he released a single by an artist going by the name of "Steve Soul," who was, in fact, James Brown. The record, 'A Talk With The News', was really just a promotional single with different cuts of James Brown tracks mixed in to answer some pre-recorded questions. Yet, in his article on the history of cut and paste which appeared in *Big Daddy* magazine, Neil McMillan says of 'A Talk With The News', that "despite occasional comic misfires, it's easy to see how the humorous interplay between spoken word and sampled excerpt sets the blueprint for the satirical and narrative elements not only of Steinski's cut-ups but, even if unconsciously, many a scratch DJ's acapella routines" (McMillan 2002). In fact in the notes to a double CD of early breakbeat classics called *Breaks Sessions*, it *credits* James Brown with the first "break." "What was the first break? That's a moot point. James Brown put together a couple of records credited to 'Steve Soul' in the early 1970s [sic], which were basically edits of many of his records with an announcer talking over them" (McCann 2002).

Despite his contribution to the burgeoning electronic dance music genres, Brown's work obviously existed within a much broader canon, one that is now well recognized, including other more obscure examples such as 'It's Just Begun' by the Jimmy Castor Bunch, 'Apache' by the Incredible Bongo Band, 'Shack Up' by Banbarra and Babe Ruth's 'The Mexican' (Brewster and Broughton 2001). Nevertheless, no other artist had their catalogue pilfered to the same degree as Brown's. It is testament to how his work would stand up over time that he would provide one of the most enduring influences on this style of artistic production, from the late 1960s to the present day.

Irrational Cuts

Not only did it provide for great dance music, but the process of subjecting records to the creative potential of the "irrational cut" enacted a new relationship to time, and a new presentation of history, in turn. For the extrication of the record's breakbeats would have the added bonus of symbolically dislocating the narratives of the records in which they were once contained; as once "rational," linear musical movements were delivered their full potential through irrational connection. Instead of the totalization and projection inherent to the conventions of the action-image, these new musical styles would pursue the application of irrational cuts as a means to court the affective potential of indeterminacy, a practice just as common to both the disco and hip-hop styles of the time:

> Beatmatching, cuts and blends (or "running" records, as Pete calls it) were required skills on the gay scene thanks to pioneers like Terry Noel, Francis Grasso, Steve D'Acquisto and Michael Cappello. Grandmaster Flowers, who'd been playing since 1967, as well as Plummer, Maboya and Pete Jones himself, deserve credit for developing the same skills at the same time and – crucial to our story – for showing them off to the wide world of greater New York. 'They would say that Flowers was a mixer and I was a chopper," says Pete, describing Grandmaster Flowers' style as being closest to the DJs in the gay clubs. "Flowers was an expert mixer. He didn't chop too many of the records, he would blend. Plummer was a mixer also, but I liked to chop, I liked to get the beat BANG! BANG! – I loved to chop. Even before I had a cueing system, I liked to chop them records up" (Brewster and Broughton 2001).

It is in service of the ever present "now" or a series of "presents" that informs such "mixing and chopping." This wilful cultivation of irrational cuts coalesces into a sense of immersion, enacting a reversal of movement and time similar to that which Deleuze defines as the shift from movement-image to time-image. Within this reversal, "time is no longer the measure of movement but movement is the perspective of time" (Deleuze 1989: 22). In comparison to the more closed form of the traditional pop song that might be understood as a "whole" (verse/chorus/bridge etc.), the irrational composition of the post-soul aesthetic was dedicated to a more open form of composition. This courting of the irrational cut had the effect of throwing the "common sense" linkages associated with the more traditional forms of composition into disarray.

Thus, the indeterminacy of the irrational cut opens up time to the chaos of the "outside," where this outside might be perceived as the virtual pool of time in all of its potential juxtapositions of past, present and future. This openness to the virtual possibility of time promoted through these irrational cuts and indeterminate relationships might be compared against the more sequential and logical linear unification of chronological time. For the indeterminate, open composition is full of virtual temporal alterity, a process demonstrated for example in the Dadaist cut-up technique inherited by Brion Gysin and subsequently passed on to William S. Burroughs. This aleatory process of creation was enacted through the dissection of various texts, which, when re-assembled, would produce new and unforeseen relationships and assemblages. Inspired by cut-up, Burroughs commented that, "[p]erhaps events are pre-written and pre-recorded and when you cut word lines the future leaks out" (Burroughs in Odier and Burroughs 1974: 28).

Through the pursuit of "irrational cuts," new and unforeseen connections that might produce possible futures do, in fact, leak out. For the irrational cut uncovers an array of virtual temporalities that exist outside of the rigid "totality" of sequential, privileged instants. This new irrational relationship to time will prove essential to electronic dance music production, because it is in irrational connection that becoming emerges, freed as it is from the more individual, subjective forms of duration:

> Time's direct image is not time in itself, but rather the force of virtuality and becoming, or what remains both outside of, yet in reserve and immanent to, our contemporary modes of existence. The irrational interval does not signify or represent; it resists. And it restores a belief in the virtual as a site where choice has yet to be determined, a reservoir of unthought yet immanent possibilities and modes of existence (Rodowick 1997: 204).

The groove-based music of the post-soul era, characterized by the "indeterminacy" that ruptures a linear causality of action–reaction, drives the heterogeneous becomings that emerge from "irrational" relationships formed through the juxtaposition of musical texts. Framing such musical practice as a transcendence of the sensory-motor logic of action–reaction was surely not in the forefront of the minds of post-soul musicians, even if they did nevertheless arrive at a similar aesthetic approach in their own intuitive way. The desire to dance is to seek sanctuary from the banality of a common-sense chronological time that marked the menial, low-paid jobs that employed them between trips to the dance floor. The only way to transcend this environment is the groove, which would always be of importance to any minor culture whose everyday life was so overwhelmingly imposed upon by the dominant forms of hegemonic time.

The Post-Soul Any-Space-Whatever

It is the imposition of chronos as hegemonic time that enforces the lack of movement, and is constituent of the existential circumstances of a post-soul generation who are left to ponder a future when their political options (in the traditional sense) are exhausted. While the 1970s were bad, Reagan's regressive social policies of the 1980s seemed to have been deliberately designed to punish those who had dared rise up during the soul movement. Once-vibrant communities would fall into ruin and simply be left that way, based on the lack of any coherent policy to redress the destruction of infrastructure. Given this situation, Nelson George would comment that the generation characterized here as post-soul, grew up "seeing negative change" (George in Barrett and Thomson [dir.] *Make It Funky*). The post-soul malaise would only be reinforced by these visible reminders of soul's apparent failure which further contributes to the proliferation of disconnected spaces that exacerbates the decline in action motivation. Correlative with the example given by Deleuze, we might address these places as the *any-space-whatever*, where the latter reflects Deleuze's idiosyncratic transformation of Augé's concept of the "non-place." These *any-space-whatevers* are responsible for the ruptures to the normal sequential logic of the movement-image's action-image and constitute the more disjointed relationship to time/space of the time-image aesthetic. Furthermore, in Deleuze's cinematic example, such dislocated spaces will constitute the foundation of the production of a cinema based around the more anonymous, transitional spaces of these any-space-whatevers:

> ... after the war, a proliferation of such spaces could be seen both in film sets and in exteriors, under various influences. The first, independent of cinema, was the post-war situation with its towns demolished or being reconstructed, its waste grounds, its shanty towns, and even in places where the war had not penetrated, its undifferentiated urban tissue, its vast unused places, docks, warehouses, heaps of girders and scrap iron. Another, more specific to the cinema as we shall see, arose from a crisis of the action-image: the characters were found less and less in sensory-motor "motivating" situations, but rather in a state of strolling, of sauntering or of rambling which defined pure optical and sound situations. The action-image then tended to shatter, while the determinate locations were blurred, letting any-spaces-whatever rise up where the modern affects of fear, detachment, but also freshness, extreme speed and interminable waiting were developing (Deleuze 1986: 120–21).

Deleuze's transformation of the *any-space-whatever*, "[i]n contrast to Augé . . . rather than being an homogenizing and de-singularizing force . . . is a condition for the emergence of uniqueness and singularities" and a catalyst for productivity (Bell 1997). Ever the optimist, Deleuze prizes this non-place for its unique becoming-potential, "a space of virtual conjunction, grasped as pure locus of the possible" (Deleuze 1986: 109) and that from the post-War proliferation of any-space-whatevers a vibrant time-image cinema will emerge. As Brian Massumi writes: "*Cherish derelict spaces*. They are holes in habit, what cracks in the existing order appear to be from the molar perspective . . . The derelict space is a zone of indeterminacy that bodies-in-becoming may make their own" (Massumi 1992: 104).

To emerge from intolerable circumstances, creative resources must be found, and driving the production of a creative time-image music was this proliferation of derelict spaces that beckoned their transformation:

> This is in fact the clearest aspect of the modern voyage. It happens in any-space-whatever –marshalling yard, disused warehouse, and the undifferentiated fabric of the city – in opposition to action, which most often unfolded in the qualified space-time of the old realism . . . it is a question

of undoing space, as well as the story, the plot or action (Deleuze 1986: 208).

The proliferation of any-space-whatevers in the United States, and beyond, prompts a series of unique artistic responses, where emphatic groove-oriented forms of composition would be summoned to counteract the sheer banality of these spaces. These any-space-whatevers not only gave rise to block parties and warehouse raves the world over, but emerged from the equally disconnected spaces that produced sound system culture in the ghettos of Trenchtown, or the rigid electronic synthesis of disaffected post-War Germany, and heard, for example, in the music of Kraftwerk.

That the irrational music at the heart of the post-soul generation would emerge from ghettos (hip-hop) and the "disused warehouses" (house and "rave" cultures) provides a significant correspondence with the any-space-whatever conditions that would drive Deleuze's cinematic forms. As he discusses in great detail in *Cinema 2*, the more indeterminate concepts of time and space facilitated through the *voyages* and *any-space-whatevers* are the result of the breakdown in the "qualified space-time of the old realism" formerly driven by an "organic" sensory-motor connection. As a product of this decline in the logical flow of action and chronological time, the resulting time-image aesthetic will interrupt these more common-sense notions of time and space, and, by extension, present an unconscious revision of temporality. It is this renegotiation of historical time, which will become intrinsic to musical practices such as DJing and sampling, and that might reflect a new musical "image of thought," one that transpires from disenfranchised urban populations of any-space-whatevers that arose as visible, everyday reminders of the failure of the political goals of the post-soul period, such as the riots proceeding from the assassination of Dr. King:

> *US News and World Report* noted on November 13, 1967, 101 major riots had occurred in US cities, killing 130 people and injuring 3,673. The damage would total $714.8 million ... King's assassination quickly upped the ante: more cities were paralysed, more people hurt, more homes and businesses and communities destroyed (Rose 1990: 67).

The problem was that these sites were often never rebuilt.

Yet, in a manner exemplary of Deleuze's any-space-whatever, we witness an emergent hip-hop culture from the ghettos of the South Bronx. As Tricia Rose recounts in *Black Noise* (1994), the borough was legally decimated under the direction of legendary planner Robert Moses, so that

> [i]n 1959, city, state, and federal authorities began the implementation of his planned Cross-Bronx Expressway that cut directly through the center of the most heavily populated working-class areas in the Bronx. As once stable neighborhoods were depopulated, property values plummeted and the community economically and socially depleted (Rose 1994: 30).

As conditions worsened in the late 1960s to mid-1970s landlords turned their properties wholesale over to professional slumlords that only continued to exacerbate the erosion of any kind of stable community (Rose 1994: 33). Given that such "urban renewal" projects as the Cross-Bronx Expressway could have been modified to minimize destruction, such projects actually produced the "slums" out of the working-class community housing in the area (Rose 1994: 31).

Within these derelict spaces, Brown was a ubiquitous presence. Their affective and transformative capacities ensured that his pioneering grooves were a feature of dance music cultures the world over. As Grandmaster Flash attests in his recent autobiography, the death of Brown in 2006 had an enormous effect on the post-soul generation:

> I sat there for the rest of the day, just lost in my thoughts. JB wasn't just *the* Godfather, he was my Godfather. God had spoken to me through his music – the maddening basslines and impossibly revolutionary rhythms. God had shown me how to pick the individual bits and pieces of instrumentation apart, thanks to James Brown's songs. My own father wasn't always around. But James Brown was (Grandmaster Flash and Ritz 2008: 242).

From the any-space-whatever of the South Bronx, Flash spoke for a generation who saw Brown as a consistent force of existential sustenance. This might explain the continuing popularity of James Brown's music as a sample source, as it conjures up that pure affective relation that punctures the rational time and space of hegemonic domination. Brown's squeals and grunts are now ubiquitous, as a grunt or a well-timed "Good God!" are sampled for their capacity to act as affective intensity, standing for themselves, not tied to narrative. Furthermore these punctuating screams take over where language fails. A James Brown sample extricated from the past and reiterated through the music of DJ or sampler allows for a series of transversal relations that transforms any punctual or static past into the flow of the past.

Emphasizing the difference between the punctual and the transversal is the best way to pursue the ensuing shift from the sequential to the serial, or from representation to "nomad thought" (which might be understood as the counter-hegemonic strategies of the minor). We could cite this compositional process as the shift towards the non-linear and the serial found in remix culture. Through their aesthetic practices, the problematic takes precedence over the space of determination. This reminds us of a relationship between minor art and seriality noted by Rodowick, "Few have noted that most of Deleuze's examples of 'serial' cinema come from 'hybrid' and postcolonial filmmakers, including Pierre Perrault, Glauber Rocha, Ousmane Sembene, the Los Angeles school of African American filmmakers, and many others" (Rodowick 1997: 140).

The serial, break-driven music of the post-soul aesthetic not only introduces new transversal relations between constituent texts, but the reterritorialization of old texts into new music possibility problematizes the relationship between model and copy, as it changes our relationship to time. If, for example, the DJ plays a segment from one of Brown's old records as part of a new mix, it falsifies the official history of the original, as it juxtaposes it with that recollection of the "original" track, brought into the present; a practice that takes back the power over representation. This is perhaps why the powers of the false, inherent to "bastardization," proved just as vital to the post-soul aesthetic as it did to a time-image cinema; it is a manipulation of the official representation of history, and the chronological time that constituted that history. Perhaps this is why Deleuze finds the crystalline time-image problematic (Deleuze 1989: 174) because it eschews the linearity of chronos, to expose us instead to time's co-existent dimensions; the concurrent unfolding of past, present and future in each and every instant, of which practices such as sampling and DJing make such great artistic use.

These "irrational" styles of time-image music production can be perceived as "crystalline," because each time a breakbeat is emancipated, it allows the line of time from which it originally emerged to be emancipated in the process as well. Old soul records can be seen as a big pool of virtual past, where each and every moment of these records alludes to a potential future that can be brought out through the repetition of these refrains. These "images" of the past are delivered back as pure blocks of pragmatic potential, a process that, in turn, re-consolidates its relationship with the virtual. This process of falsification requires an infidelity to "faithful" representation, and through the interplay of representation and appearance art brings out the power of the virtual; it turns the determined time/space of the historical narrative into a (productive) temporal problematization.

Representation and Appearance

As Paul Patton discusses in his essay, "Anti-Platonism and Art" (1994), much postmodern art "works" through the play of representation and appearance, where, "[t]he shock value in some cases derives from the fact that what is reproduced is the appearance of earlier artwork themselves" (Patton 1994: 142). By way of demonstration, Patton will discuss the work of artist, Sherrie Levine, whose oeuvre consisted of the rephotographing or repainting of all or part of works by earlier artists as typical of this play of representation and appearance. Her work, he says, deliberately subverts the traditional notions of a meaningful original and less meaningful copy as it brings the "original" into a new relationship with its copy, one that will directly challenge our concepts of representation and appearance: ". . . the conception of the artist's task: the reproduction of appearances rather than their representation" (Patton 1994: 142).

Patton's discussion of this play of representation and appearance can be instructive for thinking about another apparently postmodern phenomenon, that of sampling. The digital replication at the heart of sampling practice will necessarily transform the history and context of the music that is repeated. As Clare Colebrook comments here, "the essence is repeated or affirmed, not by a repetition of something that is the same; repetition is difference. For what we repeat is the power of each event to affirm itself over and over again in different ways. Art is crucially tied to difference and repetition" (Colebrook 2002: 92). The artwork that embraces such difference should not be conceived in terms of a divergence from an original model but should instead be considered as that power to repeatedly produce new forms:

> For production, at least in one of its senses, essentially involves the transformation of a raw material into a product. It is therefore inseparable from the creation or the institution of a difference where none existed before. The means of production, which include the artist's conceptual as well as physical materials and techniques, are the means by which this difference is created. By contrast, representation, at least in one of its senses, essentially involves the maintenance of an identity; the reappearance of that which appeared before (Patton 1994: 142).

This is why representation is not at the heart of artistic endeavour, but as already proposed in Chapter 1, art is instead concerned with the production of affects and percepts, or the bloc of sensations found within the artwork. These sensations create relations that connect bodies rather than divide them. The powers of the false are in such ways dedicated to the creation of new perspectives and new thoughts that might arise out of the juxtaposition of representation and appearance. For the re-appearance of the work as simulacrum brings out a new-found serial relationship, as the original must now contend with its copy, and forces both outside of the hierarchy of images. Through the unleashing of the simulacra, the forger creates a new plane of time where the copy exists as an accepted original and forges new relations around the "copied" work. Through practices such as DJing and sampling we witness how simulacra are productively utilized by minor musical producers to extract a co-existent dimension of the temporal, snatched from under the nose of the hegemonic chronos in which it once floundered.

Powers of the False

This play of representation and appearance is the function of the "powers of the false." Instead of categorizing the simulacrum in a Platonic fashion – as the poor copy – Deleuze's "powers of the false" give the simulacrum a reality of its own. It frees us from the Platonic hierarchy of images, which starts with the original as model, the copy as the faithful reproduction of the model, and, finally, external to this relationship, the simulacrum as the bad reproduction of the original model (Deleuze 1990b: 253–65). While the simulacrum possesses an extrinsic resemblance to the model, it is never intrinsically or absolutely connected to it and thus enables the simulacrum to establish its own reality. Freed from the shadows of a more authentic model, the Deleuzean simulacrum will generate becomings which are just as real and valid as any "original," and, as Deleuze will argue, "if the simulacrum still has a model, it is another model, a model of the Other (l'autre)" (Deleuze 1990b: 258). As such, the powers of the false bestow simulation with the power of its own subversive becoming. "In short, there is in the simulacrum a becoming-mad, or a becoming unlimited . . . a becoming always other, a becoming subversive" (Deleuze 1990b: 258–59).

The Deleuzean powers of the false, then, are not the pursuit of the untrue, and do not exist in some dialectical relation to an established truth. As inherent to the time-image (or crystalline regime), the productive power of the simulacrum enables the pursuit of difference over that which can be identified as real or true, as D. N. Rodowick has neatly summarized in the following passage:

> In the organic regime, truth can only be found, discovered, or described. But there is a "falsifying" narration, Nietzschean in inspiration, which does away with the opposition of true and false and instead creates truth positively. The primary question for Deleuze is how thought can be kept moving, not toward a predetermined end, but toward the new and unforeseen in terms of what Bergson calls the Open or "creative evolution." Thus the organic and crystalline regimes are qualitatively different with respect to how they answer the question "What is thinking?" For the former it is the discovery of concepts through negation, repetition, and identity toward ever more self-identical Being; for the latter it is the creation of concepts through difference and non-identity in a continually open Becoming (Rodowick 1997: 85).

We can argue that the samples of James Brown, as simulacra, are mobilized into production of new musical texts, which give these refrains a life of their own, unencumbered by their subordination to some notion of original identity. This is how art is creative, or how it might constitute a "war zone." Just as "an insect that mimics a leaf does so not to meld with the vegetable state of its surrounding milieu, but to reenter the higher realm of predatory animal warfare on a new footing" (Massumi 1987). The fact that fraught relationship between the original and copy is always ready to be exploited for its power is why this relationship is so actively policed by copyright law, which is simply a testament to the inherent power of the simulacrum.

Brown's refrains proved vital catalysts in the minor's "war" on the representation of official history, its powers of the false duly summoned into battle through the simulacrum, as the official version of history (the model) is thrown into the chaosmos of virtual alterity (or the time contained in the present's co-existent past) through the copy. It is through these powers of the false that the *time* of a time-image cinema will begin to be "opened up," as it finds its own methods of confronting chaos "in order to rediscover, to restore the infinite" (Deleuze and Guattari 1994: 197). Art's power is derived from this rediscovery of the vast virtual potential of the infinite, or the possibility of eternal difference. In terms of an application of this idea to the practices of DJing and sampling culture, we might say that through the repetition of the James Brown sample, the original is submitted to its own eternal difference, rather than merely existing as real or true in any ideal sense. Of course, the State sanctioned copyright law conspires against this power, and the creative potential of contemporary sampling culture or remix culture remain the property of Platonism.

But rather than being perceived as the poor copy, the sample should be seen as the means to free the alterity and transversality inherent in the musical assemblage of the "original." In terms of the pragmatics of the sample as simulacrum for itself, the point is, who cares – does it work? That is, does it make us respond, react, dance?

For example, an album such as Public Enemy's *It Takes a Nation of Millions to Hold Us Back* is considered "not only the greatest hip-hop album of all time, it's one of the greatest albums in all the world of music" (The Source 1998: 174) even though Brown's refrains are foundational to its composition. As Musik was to remark in its 2002 article on "The Top 50 Dance Albums of All Time," Public Enemy's *It Takes a Nation of Millions to Hold Us Back* (the highest rated hip-hop album on the list at No. 19) was "the sound of the apocalypse, as orchestrated by James Brown" (Musik 2002: 45). Here, for example, are a few of the James Brown samples used on the album: 'Rebel Without a Pause' (samples from James Brown's 'Get Up Offa That Thing' and 'Funky Drummer'); 'Bring the Noise' (samples James Brown's 'Funky Drummer'); 'Don't

Believe the Hype' (samples James Brown's 'Escape-ism' and 'I Got Ants In My Pants'); 'Terminator X to the Edge of Panic' (samples James Brown's 'Funky Drummer' and 'Get Up, Get Into It, Get Involved'); 'Night of the Living Baseheads' (samples James Brown's 'Soul Power Pt. 1' and 'Get Up, Get Into It, Get Involved'); 'Caught, Can We Get A Witness?' (samples James Brown's 'Soul Power Pt. 1' and James Brown produced/Bobby Byrd track 'Hot Pants . . . I'm Coming, I'm Coming, I'm Coming'); 'Prophets of Rage' (samples James Brown's 'Cold Sweat'); 'Party for Your Right to Fight' (samples James Brown's 'Get Up, Get Into It, Get Involved' and James Brown produced/Bobby Byrd track 'I Know You Got Soul'); 'Cold Lampin' with Flavor' ('I Know You Got Soul').

The positive reception *It Takes a Nation of Millions to Hold Us Back* has received over the years can only be the result of a suspension of judgement of the simulacrum. Instead of negating the connections made, or assimilating them back into an original identity, we might instead look at productive relations to emerge from this process. How could Public Enemy's album constitute such an acute commentary on its contemporary politics, or conjure a fidelity to its imminent soundscape, when most of its music came from the past? Yet it still works, and is lauded to this day, as it maintains its vitality through this patchwork series of sample linkages. In short, an embrace of the simulacrum is intellectually problematic, and all the more productive for this reason. The play between representation and appearance is how the text "works." As Deleuze will remind us, we should keep in mind the Nietzschean idea that "the 'true world' does not exist, and, if it did, would be inaccessible, impossible to describe, and, if it could be described, would be useless, superfluous" (Deleuze 1989: 137).

To think in terms of truth is to be implicitly bound up in the dogmatic maintenance of identity. Forgers and outlaws, like the post-soul musicians of this chapter, are necessary to aid the construction of the new by operating outside the law, resisting common sense and moral judgements, and thus even the "truth" itself. The minor must "forge" new connections to extricate their representation out of the hands of the State. As Deleuze will say: "the moment the master, or the colonizer, proclaims 'there have never been people here,' the missing people are a becoming, they invent themselves, in shanty towns and camps, or in ghettos, in new conditions of struggle to which a necessarily political art must contribute" (Deleuze 1989: 217).

Yet there are limits to this practice as well. The work of art, whether a sample of James Brown or otherwise, is resigned to cliché when the repetition of the simulacrum is no longer constitutive of "the means" of the "war zone" but rather becomes an end in itself. That is, if the practice simply mimics rather than reflects an apprehension of a minor temporality. For Deleuze, the cliché is responsible for the automatism of our everyday lives, because, "[a] cliché is a sensory-motor image of the thing" (Deleuze 1989: 20). When LA Style decried that James Brown was dead, it was because the situation arose where the James Brown sample was used *because it is James Brown*, as a trend, as imitation, rather than as a post-soul inspired historical emancipation of alterity. It missed an important point of DJing and sampling culture which made use of new economies of the musical refrain to overturn majoritarian control of the truths of history. They replace the falsity of official discourse with their own. New forms and approaches to music beckon the invention of a people who have no affective representation – or only official representation – available to them.

Memory

Which is how we get back to the initial proposition at the outset of the book. While the heyday of unrestrained Brown sampling might have waned since the late 1980s and early 1990s, this does not mean that it has stopped. With his catalogue of 800+ songs, the DJs are just a little more cunning about the way they use his refrains, often subjecting them to time stretching and various effects to disguise them. Given the widespread manipulation of Brown's music in the form of the many samples that have appeared time and again, whether 'Funky Drummer', 'Think (About It)', or 'Funky President', to name a few of the most persistent, one wonders just how much more currency is to be gained by their continued usage? Perhaps the best that might be achieved is that they might "parody the cliché" (Deleuze 1986: 211) even if this is, in itself, not enough to "disturb the sensory-motor connections" (Deleuze 1989: 22) and forge new methods of becoming.

While the proliferation of cliché might be curtailed through copyright law, the state is also hampered by the relative speed of minority practice. By the time the law begins clamping down on a particular practice, such as sampling, chances are that any artistic revolution has already taken place long before. The worst effect of this State co-option is not so much to be found in the exploitation of the economic gains made through the minor, but rather how such practices more generally serve to reiterate majoritarian power. It is not only a question of those institutions which enforce the law, but of a power they have over – and through – "official" representation. On this point Deleuze and Guattari will distinguish between "memory" and "Memory" in regard to the minor: "Of course, the child, the woman, the black have memories; but the Memory that collects those memories is still a virile majoritarian agency treating them as 'childhood memories,' as conjugal, or colonial memories" (Deleuze and Guattari 1988: 293). Demonstrative of this State-sanctioned Memory are the attempts by record companies to co-opt the memories of the minor, whether this is through authorship, publishing as copyrights and so on.

There is much more to be said for an increasingly litigious society and its continued restriction of practices such as sampling. In fact there is much to be learned from a wilful "bastardization" and we should turn our attention towards the new connections the bastard has forged in its name, rather than simply postulate its attachment to a history that neither it, nor its audience, will ever really know, nor ever really care to contemplate. To deny the bastard simulacrum its right to exist as a singular image is to maintain a concept of original identity that is dogmatic rather than creative.

It is though the copy, through bastardization, through the simulacra, that James Brown continues, unlike many of his peers, to "work." He embodies the concept of the artist who "creates a people," and a capacity for becoming where it once did not exist, even if the people he created, and the future in which they resided, were ultimately unrecognizable:

> At dinner with old friend Cliff White after accepting a special award at Britain's March 1988 DMC (Disco Mix Club) Championships, Brown betrayed confusion about a reception so rapturous White himself had been stunned. "It was quite amazing standing with him behind that curtain in the Royal Albert Hall, and seeing the place just packed with street kids! It was such a charged atmosphere. Then, when they announced 'James Brown' – which had been a well-kept secret – and pulled back the drapes, it was just like the Beatles. Pandemonium! . . . But back at the hotel," says White, "every once in a while, James would go back to the evening and say, 'But why didn't they ask me to sing? What was I really there for? Why wasn't I asked to sing a song?' He really didn't seem to know what it *meant*" (Rose 1990: 151).

Bibliography

Batey, Angus (2002). "Spin City." *Mojo* (October): 56–62.
BBC News (2006). "Stars Turn Out for Brown Funeral." BBC News (30 December 2006). http://news.bbc.co.uk/2/hi/entertainment/6219659.stm. Accessed 20 July 2011.
Beastie Boys, and Michael Heatley (1999). *Beastie Boys: In Their Own Words*. London: Omnibus Press.
Bell, Jeffrey A. (1997). "Thinking with Cinema: Deleuze and Film Theory." *Film-Philosophy* 1, no. 8. http://www.film-philosophy.com/vol1-1997/n8bell. Accessed 20 July 2011.
Bergman, Billy, and Richard Horn (1985). *Experimental Pop*. Poole: Blandford Press.
Black, Peter "Blackie" (2001). "Record Collection: The Music That Rocks Your Favourite Artists." *Rolling Stone (Australian edition)* (June): 24.
Bogue, Ronald (2005). "The Minor." In *Gilles Deleuze: Key Concepts*, ed. Charles J. Stivale, 110–20. Chesham: Acumen.
Brackett, David (1992). "James Brown's 'Superbad' and the Double-Voiced Utterance." *Popular Music* 11(3): 309–324.
Brackett, David (1995). *Interpreting Popular Music*. Cambridge and New York: Cambridge University Press.
Brackett, Nathan (1997). "The Rolling Stone 200: The Essential Rock Collection." *Rolling Stone (Australian Edition)* (July): 70.
Bradley, Lloyd (2001). *Bass Culture*. London: Penguin.
The Breaks.com. http://www.the-breaks.com/. Accessed 20 July 2011.
Brewster, Bill (1993). "The History of Dance Music." *Mixmag* 2, no. 24 (May): 66.
Brewster, Bill, and Frank Broughton (2000 [1999]). *Last Night a Dj Saved My Life: The History of the Disc Jockey*. London: Headline.
— (2001). Liner notes to *The True Life Adventures of Flash*. London: Strut.
Brown, Geoff (1996). *James Brown: Doin' It to Death*. London: Omnibus Press.
Brown, James, and Marc Eliot (2005). *I Feel Good*. New York: New American Library.
Brown, James, and Bruce Tucker (1986). *James Brown, the Godfather of Soul*. New York: Macmillan.
Christensen, Thor (2003). "James Brown Still Seeking Respect." *Knight Ridder Newspapers*, 21 May 2003. http://web.archive.org/web/20060430235617/http://members.aol.com/staritems/news.htm. Accessed 30 July 2011.
Chuck D. (1998). Liner notes to *Say It Live and Loud – Live in Dallas 08.26.68*. New York: Polygram.
Colebrook, Claire (2002). *Gilles Deleuze*. London: Routledge.
Danielsen, Anne (2006). *Presence and Pleasure: The Funk Grooves of James Brown and Parliament*. Middleton, CT: Wesleyan University Press.
Deleuze, Gilles (1986). *Cinema 1: The Movement-Image*, trans. Hugh Tomlinson and Barbara Habberjam. Minneapolis: University of Minnesota.
—(1989). *Cinema 2: The Time-Image*, trans. Hugh Tomlinson and Robert Galeta. London: Athlone Press.

— (1990a). *The Logic of Sense*, trans. Mark Lester and Charles J. Stivale. New York: Columbia University Press.
— (1990b). "Plato and the Simulacrum," trans. Mark Lester and Charles J. Stivale. In *The Logic of Sense*, ed. Constantin V. Boundas, 253–65. New York: Columbia University Press.
— (1994). *Difference and Repetition*, trans. Paul Patton. London: Athlone Press.
— (1995). *Negotiations, 1972–1990*, trans. Martin Joughin. New York: Columbia University Press.
— (1998). "Vincennes Seminar Session of May 3, 1977: On Music." *webdeleuze.com*, trans. Timothy S. Murphy. http://web.archive.org/web/20010709182647/http://www.imaginet.fr/deleuze/TXT/ENG/030577.html. Accessed 30 July 2010.
Deleuze, Gilles, and Félix Guattari (1983). *Anti-Oedipus: Capitalism and Schizophrenia*, trans. Helen R. Lane Robert Hurley and Mark Seem. Minneapolis: University of Minnesota Press.
— (1986). *Kafka: Toward a Minor Literature*, trans. Dana Polan. Minneapolis: University of Minnesota Press.
— (1988). *A Thousand Plateaus: Capitalism and Schizophrenia*, trans. Brian Massumi. London: Athlone Press.
— (1994). *What Is Philosophy?*, trans. Hugh Tomlinson and Graham Burchell. New York: Columbia University Press.
Deleuze, Gilles, and Claire Parnet (1996). "L'abécédaire de Gilles Deleuze, avec Claire Parnet (Gilles Deleuze's Abc Primer, with Claire Parnet)." *Wayne State University*, trans. Charles J. Stivale. http://www.langlab.wayne.edu/CStivale/D-G/ABC3.html. Accessed 20 July 2011.
Doggett, Peter (1997). "Live at the Apollo." *Record Collector* 216 (June): 77.
Dunayevskaya, Raya (1967). "Revisiting 'Black Power', Race and Class." *marxists.org*. http://www.marxists.org/archive/dunayevskaya/works/1967/black-power.htm. Accessed 30 July 2011.
Dyer, Richard (1997). *White*. London: Routledge.
Eliot, Marc (2005). "Introduction." In *I Feel Good*. New York: New American Library.
Fab 5 Freddy (1992). *Fresh Fly Flavor: Words and Phrases of the Hip Hop Generation*. Stamford, CT: Longmeadow Press.
Farnsworth, Philo T., Steev Hise, and Carrie McLaren (2002). "Stay Free's Illegal Art Compilation Cd." *illegalart.org*. http://www.illegal-art.org/audio/liner.html. Accessed 20 July 2011.
Fernando Jr, S. H. (1999). "Back in the Day: 1975–1979." In *The Vibe History of Hip Hop (1st edition)*, ed. Alan Light, 13–21. New York: Three Rivers Press.
Flaxman, Gregory (2000). "Introduction." In *The Brain is the Screen: Deleuze and the Philosophy of Cinema*, ed. Gregory Flaxman, 1–50. Minneapolis: University of Minnesota Press.
Foulsham, Dom (1993). "Sixty with a Bullet." *Blues and Soul* 638 (25 May–7 June): 26–28.
Gaunt, Kyra D. (2004). "Translating Double-Dutch to Hip-Hop." In *That's the Joint! The Hip-Hop Studies Reader*, ed. Murray Forman and Mark Anthony Neal, 251–63. New York: Taylor and Francis.
George, Nelson (1988). *The Death of Rhythm and Blues*. New York: Pantheon Books.
— (1992). *Buppies, B-boys, Baps and Bohos: Notes on Post-Soul Black Culture*. New York: Harper Collins.
— (1999). *Hip Hop America*. New York: Penguin Books.
— (2004). *Post-Soul Nation: The Explosive, Contradictory, Triumphant, and Tragic 1960s as Experienced by African Americans*. New York: Viking Books.

George, Nelson and Alan Leeds (2008). *The James Brown Reader: 50 Years of Writing About the Godfather of Soul*. New York: Plume.
Gilbert, Jeremy (2004a). "Becoming-Music: The Rhizomatic Moment of Improvisation." In *Deleuze and Music*, ed. Ian Buchanan and Marcel Swiboda, 118–39. Edinburgh: Edinburgh University Press.
— (2004b). "Signifying Nothing: 'Culture', 'Discourse' and the Sociality of Affect." *Culture Machine* 6. http://culturemachine.net/index.php/cm/issue/view/1. Accessed 30 July 2011.
Gilbert, Jeremy, and Ewan Pearson (1999). *Discographies: Dance Music, Culture, and the Politics of Sound*. New York: Routledge.
Gilroy, Paul (1993). *The Black Atlantic: Modernity and Double Consciousness*. Cambridge, MA: Harvard University Press.
— (2004). "It's a Family Affair." In *That's the Joint! The Hip-Hop Studies Reader*, ed. Murray Forman and Mark Anthony Neal, 87–103. New York: Taylor and Francis.
Gladstone, Eric, Russell Simins, and John "Jabo" Starks (1997). "The Man with the 'Good Foot'." *Grand Royal* 6: 42–44.
Gladstone, Eric, Russell Simins and Clyde Stubblefield (1997). "The Man They Call The Funky Drummer." *Grand Royal* 6: 40–41.
Goldman, Albert (1992 [1968]). "James Brown=Black Power." In *Sound Bites*. New York: Turtle Bay Books.
Goodwin, Andrew (1990). "Sample and Hold: Pop Music in the Digital Age of Reproduction." In *On Record: Rock, Pop, and the Written Word*, ed. Simon Frith and Andrew Goodwin, 258–74. New York: Pantheon Books.
Gourevitch, Philip (2002). "Mr. Brown: On the Road with his Bad Self." *New Yorker*, 29 July: 46–65.
Grandmaster Flash, and David Ritz (2008). *The Adventures of Grandmaster Flash*. New York: Broadway Books.
Guattari, Félix (1995). *Chaosmosis: An Ethico-Aesthetic Paradigm*, trans. Paul Bains and Julian Pefanis. Sydney: Power Publications.
Guralnick, Peter (1971). *Feel Like Going Home: Portraits in Blues and Rock 'n' Roll*. London: Penguin Books.
— (1986). *Sweet Soul Music: Rhythm and Blues and the Southern Dream of Freedom*. New York: Harper and Row.
Haralambos, Michael (1974). *Right On: From Blues to Soul in Black America*. London: Eddison Press.
Harrington, Jon, and John Paul Jones (2002). "Keeping up with the Jones: John Paul Jones Speaks to Jon Harrington." *Mojo Collections* (Spring): 16–17.
Hay, Fred J. (2003). "Music Box Meets the Toccoa Band: The Godfather of Soul in Appalachia." *Black Music Research Journal* 23, no. 1-2: 103–33.
Headlam, Dave (2002). "Appropriations of Blues and Gospel in Popular Music." In *The Cambridge Companion to Blues and Gospel Music*, ed. Alan Moore, 158–87. Cambridge: Cambridge University Press.
Hirshey, Gerri (1984). *Nowhere to Run: The Story of Soul Music*. London: Macmillan.
— (1985). *Nowhere to Run: The Story of Soul Music*. London: Pan Books.
Hoskyns, Barney (2004). "Super Bad." *Uncut* (March): 68–71.
Jones, LeRoi (1963). *Blues People: Negro Music in White America*. New York: W. Morrow.
— (1967). *Black Music*. New York: William Morrow and Co.

Jones, Trina (2000). "Shades of Brown: The Law of Skin Color." *Duke Law School*. http://web.archive.org/web/20070112211915/http://www.law.duke.edu/journals/dlj/articles/dlj49p1487.htm. Accessed 30 July 2011.

Keyes, Cheryl L. (2002). *Rap Music and Street Consciousness*. Urbana, IL: University of Illinois Press.

Kofsky, Frank (1970). *Black Nationalism and the Revolution in Music*. New York: Pathfinder Press.

Kumar, Shiv K. (1962). *Bergson and the Stream of Consciousness Novel*. London and Glasgow: Blackie and Son.

Lascaibar, Juice (TC-5) (1998). "Hip-Hop 101 Respect the Architects of Your History." *The Source* 100 (January): 26–27.

Law, John (1997). "Heterogeneities." Centre for Science Studies, Lancaster University. http://www.lancs.ac.uk/fass/sociology/papers/law-heterogeneities.pdf. Accessed 30 July 2011.

Lechte, John (1994). *Fifty Key Contemporary Thinkers*. London: Routledge.

Leeds, Alan (2007). Liner notes to *James Brown: The Singles Volume 2: 1960–1963*. Universal.

Lethem, Jonathon (2006). "Being James Brown." *Rolling Stone*, 12 June 2006. http://web.archive.org/web/20070106140717/http://www.rollingstone.com/news/story/10533775/being_james_brown/4. Accessed 30 July 2011.

Lyotard, Jean-François (1984). *The Postmodern Condition: A Report on Knowledge*, trans. G. Bennington and B. Massumi. Minneapolis: University of Minnesota Press.

Massumi, Brian (1987). "Realer than Real: The Simulacrum according to Deleuze and Guattari." http://www.anu.edu.au/HRC/first_and_last/works/realer.htm. Accessed 20 July 2011.

— (1992). *A User's Guide to Capitalism and Schizophrenia: Deviations from Deleuze and Guattari*. Cambridge, MA: MIT Press.

— (1996). "The Autonomy of Affect." In *Deleuze: A Critical Reader*, ed. Paul Patton, 217–39. Oxford: Blackwell.

Maycock, James (2003). "Death or Glory." *Mojo* 116 (July): 66–74.

McCann, Ian (2002). Liner notes to *Breaks Sessions*. London: Union Square.

McMillan, Neil (2002). "Cut up or Shut up (an Edited History of Cut'n'paste)." *jahsonic.com*. http://www.jahsonic.com/NeilMcMillan.html Accessed 20 July 2011.

Middleton, Richard (1996). "Over and Over: Notes towards a Politics of Repetition." http://web.archive.org/web/20090305072046/http://www2.rz.hu-berlin.de/fpm/texte/middle.htm Accessed 11 September 2005.

Morgan, Robert P. (1991). *Twentieth-Century Music: A History of Musical Style in Modern Europe and America*. New York and London: W.W. Norton and Co.

Moulton, Tom, Bill Brewster and Frank Broughton (1998). "Interview with Tom Moulton, 30th September 1998." *djhistory.com*. http://web.archive.org/web/20080404032855/http://www.djhistory.com/djhistory/archiveInterviewDisplay.php?interview_id=16 Accessed 30 July 2011.

Musik (2002). "The Top 50 Dance Albums of All Time." *Musik* (February): 41–51.

Neal, Mark Anthony (2002). *Soul Babies: Black Popular Culture and the Post-Soul Aesthetic*. New York and London: Routledge.

Odier, Daniel, and William S. Burroughs (1974). *The Job: Interview with William Burroughs*. New York: Grove Press.

Ogg, Alex and Upshal, David (1999). *The Hip-Hop Years: A History of Rap*. London and Basingstoke: Channel 4 Books.

Bibliography 155

Palmer, Robert (1996). "A Brand New Bag." In *Dancing in the Street*, 238–57. London: BBC Books.

Patton, Paul (1994). "Anti-Platonism and Art." In *Gilles Deleuze and the Theater of Philosophy*, ed. Constantin V. Boundas and Dorothea Olkowski, 141–56. New York and London: Routledge.

Patton, Tracey Owens (2006). "Hey Girl, Am I More Than My Hair? African American Women and their Struggles with Beauty, Body Image, and Hair." *NWSA Journal* 18.2 (Summer 2006): 24–51.

Payne, Jim (1996). *Give the Drummers Some!: The Great Drummers of R&B, Funk and Soul*. Katonah, NY and Miami, FL: Face the Music Productions, Warner Bros. Publications.

Perry, L. S., and L. Bradley (2002). "Respect!" *Mojo* (March): 51–95.

Poschardt, Ulf (1998). *DJ Culture*, trans. Shaun Whiteside. London: Quartet Books.

Rajchman, John (2000). *The Deleuze Connections*. Cambridge, MA and London: MIT Press.

Reighley, Kurt B. (2000). *Looking for the Perfect Beat: The Art and Culture of the DJ*. New York: MTV/Pocket Books.

Reynolds, Simon (1999). *Generation Ecstasy: Into the World of Techno and Rave Culture*. New York: Routledge.

Rhodes, Don (2009). *Say It Loud! My Memories of James Brown Soul Brother No.1*. Guilford, CT: Globe Piquot Press.

Rodowick, D. N. (1997). *Gilles Deleuze's Time Machine*. Durham, NC and London: Duke University Press.

Rose, Cynthia (1990). *Living in America: The Soul Saga of James Brown*. London: Serpent's Tail.

Rose, Tricia (1994). *Black Noise: Rap Music and Black Culture in Contemporary America*. Hanover and London: Wesleyan University Press.

Rowland, Matt (2002). "For Sweet People from Sweet Charles." In *Wax Poetics Anthology Volume 1*, 43–55. New York: Wax Poetics Books.

Sharp, Chris (2000). "Jungle: Modern States of Mind." In *Modulations : A History of Electronic Music: Throbbing Words on Sound*, ed. Peter Shapiro, 130–55. New York: Caipirinha Productions.

Sidran, Ben (1995 [1971]). *Black Talk*. Edinburgh: Payback Press.

Smith, Daniel W. (1996). "Deleuze's Theory of Sensation: Overcoming the Kantian Duality." In *Deleuze: A Critical Reader*, ed. Paul Patton, 29–56. Oxford: Blackwell.

Snead, James A. (1998 [1981]). "Repetition as a Figure of Black Culture." In *The Jazz Cadence of American Culture*, ed. Robert G. O'Meally, 62–81. New York: Columbia University Press.

The Source (1998). "Best of the Best: The Source 100 Hip-Hop Survey." *The Source: The Magazine of Hip-Hop Music, Culture and Politics* 100 (January): 167–205.

Steuer, Eric (2004). "The Remix Masters." *WiredNews.com*. http://www.wirednews.com/wired/archive/12.11/beastie.html. Accessed 20 July 2011.

Stubblefield, Clyde (2003). Interview on *The Original*. Nardis Music/Liquid8.

Sullivan, James (2009). *The Hardest Working Man: How James Brown Saved the Soul of America*. New York: Gotham Books.

Szwed, John F. (1999). "The Real Old School." In *The Vibe History of Hip Hop*, ed. A. Light, 3–12. New York: Three Rivers Press.

Tagg, Philip (1998). "Review: Interpreting Popular Music by James Brackett." *theblackbook.net*. http://web.archive.org/web/20020619130947/http://www.theblackbook.net/acad/tagg/articles/brackrvw.html Accessed 30 July 2011.

Thompson, Ahmir "Questlove" (2001). "Give the Drummer Some" (Liner notes). *Live at the Apollo Volume 2: Deluxe Edition*, 16–17. New York: Universal Music.
Toop, David (2000). "Hip-Hop: Iron Needles of Death and a Piece of Wax." In *Modulations: A History of Electronic Music. Throbbing Words on Sound*, ed. Peter Shapiro, 88–107. New York: Caipirinha Productions.
Vincent, Rickey (1996). *Funk: The Music, the People, and the Rhythm of the One*. New York: St. Martin's Griffin.
Weinger, Harry, and Alan Leeds (1996). Liner notes to *Foundations of Funk – a Brand New Bag 1964–1969*. Polygram.
Weinger, Harry, and Cliff White (1991). "Are You Ready for Star Time?" *Star Time (Box Set Liner Notes)*, 14–44. Polygram.
Werner, Craig (2000). *A Change is Gonna Come: Music, Race and the Soul of America*. Edinburgh: Payback.
Wesley, Fred (2002). *Hit Me, Fred: Recollections of a Side Man*. Durham, NC: Duke University Press.
White, Charles (1985). *The Life and Times of Little Richard*. New York: Pocket Books.
White, Cliff (1989). Liner notes to *Roots of a Revolution*. New York: Polygram.
— (1990). Liner notes to *Messing with the Blues*. New York: Polygram.
— (2000). "Why James Brown Has Scarred Knees." Liner notes to *Ballads*. New York: Universal.
Wikipedia.com (2006). "James Brown." *Wikipedia.com*. http://en.wikipedia.org/wiki/James_Brown. Accessed 20 July 2011.
Wolk, Douglas (2004). *33 1/3 Volume 13: James Brown's Live at the Apollo*. New York and London: Continuum Books.
— (2005). "Please, Please, *Please*: James Brown's Horrible New 'Memoir'." *SeattleWeekly.com* (9 February 2005). http://www.seattleweekly.com/2005-02-09/music/please-please-please/ Accessed 30 July 2011.
Wyman, Bill (1990). *Stone Alone*. London: Viking.

Film and Broadcasts

Barrett, Sean and Hugh Thomson, dir. *Be My Baby*, from the series *Dancing in the Street: A Rock and Roll History*. BBC Video, 1996.
Barrett, Sean and Hugh Thomson, dir. *Make It Funky* from the series *Dancing in the Street: A Rock and Roll History*. BBC Video, 1996.
Binder, Steve, dir. *That Was Rock (Re-Released Title of T.A.M.I. Show)*. RBC Entertainment, 1965 (original release).
Bragg, Melvin, prod. *Lenny Henry Hunts the Funk* from the series *The South Bank Show*. London Weekend Television, 1992.
Burns, Ken, dir. *Jazz – Episode 4: "The True Welcome" 1929–1934* from the series *Jazz*. PBS Home Video, 2001.
Daniels, Mark, dir. *Classified X*. Les Sept Artes/Yeah, Inc., 1997.
Eastwood, Clint, dir. *Piano Blues* from the series *Martin Scorsese Presents the Blues*. PBS/Vulcan Productions, 2004.
Figgis, Mike, dir. *Red, White and Blues* from the series *Martin Scorsese Presents The Blues*. PBS/Vulcan Productions, 2003.
Fisher, Art, dir. *James Brown: Man to Man*. Metromedia, 1968.
Lawrence, A. dir. *Ain't It Funky Now*, from the series *Soul Deep*. BBC, 2005.

Bibliography

Lee, Iara, dir. *Modulations-Cinema for the Ear*. Caipirinha Productions, 1997.
Lerner, Murray, dir. *Electric Miles: A Different Kind of Blue*. Eagle Eye Media, 2004.
Maben, Adrian, dir. *Soul Brother No. 1*. Swallowdale Productions/RM Productions/MHF, 1978.
Mann, Michael, dir. *Ali*. Columbia Pictures, 2001.
Marre, Jeremy, dir. *James Brown: Soul Survivor* from the series *American Masters*. Universal Music, 2003.
Miller, Allan, dir. *John Cage: I Have Nothing to Say and I Am Saying It* from the series *American Masters*. Kultur Films Inc, 1990.
Peterzell, Marcus, dir. *James Brown the Godfather of Soul: A Portrait*. Goodmarc Productions/A&E Television Networks, 1995.
Priestley, Philip, dir. *The Soul of Stax*. Les Films Grain de Sable, 1994.
Reiss, Jon, dir. *Better Living through Circuitry—a Digital Odyssey into the Electronic Dance Underground*. Siren Entertainment, 2001.
Stilson, Jeff, dir. *Good Hair*. HBO Films, 2009.
Van Peebles, Melvin, dir. *Baadasssss*. Imagine Entertainment, 2003.
Van Peebles, Melvin, dir. *Sweet Sweetback's Baadasssss Song*. Xenon Entertainment Group, 1971.

Discography

A Tribe Called Quest. *Beats, Rhymes and Life*. Jive, 1996.
Afrika Bambaataa and Soul Sonic Force. 'Planet Rock'. Tommy Boy, 1982.
Afrika Bambaataa and James Brown. 'Unity (Parts 1–6)'. Tommy Boy, 1984.
Ballard, Hank. 'How You Gonna Get Respect (When You Haven't Cut Your Process Yet)?' King, 1968.
Black Eyed Peas with James Brown. 'They Don't Want Music' on *Monkey Business*. A&M, 2005.
Brown, James and the Famous Flames, 'Please, Please, Please'. Federal, 1956.
Brown, James and the Famous Flames. 'Try Me'. Federal, 1958.
Brown, James and the Famous Flames. 'I'll Go Crazy'. Federal, 1960.
Brown, James and the Famous Flames. 'Think'. Federal, 1960.
Brown, James. 'Night Train'. King, 1962.
Brown, James. 'I've Got Money'. King, 1962.
Brown, James. 'Prisoner of Love'. King, 1963.
Brown, James. 'I'm Tired But I'm Clean' on *Pure Dynamite: Live at the Royal*. King, 1964.
Brown, James. 'Oh Baby Don't You Weep (Parts 1 and 2)'. King, 1964.
Brown, James. 'Hip Bag '67' on *Live at the Garden*. King, 1967.
Brown, James. 'There Was a Time'. King, 1967.
Brown, James. 'Say It Loud—I'm Black and I'm Proud'. King, 1968.
Brown, James. 'Ain't It Funky Now (Pts 1&2)'. King, 1969.
Brown, James. 'Give It up or Turnit-a-Loose'. King, 1969.
Brown, James. 'Let a Man Come in and Do the Popcorn'. King, 1969.
Brown, James. 'Mother Popcorn'. King, 1969.
Brown, James. 'The Popcorn'. King, 1969.
Brown, James. 'Funky Drummer'. King, 1970.
Brown, James. 'Get up (I Feel Like Being a) Sex Machine (Pts 1&2)'. King, 1970.
Brown, James. 'I Don't Want Nobody to Give Nothing (Open up the Door, I'll Get It Myself) (Parts 1 and 2)' on *Sex Machine*. King/Polygram, 1970.
Brown, James. 'Escape-Ism Pt.1 and Pt.2'. Polydor, 1971.
Brown, James. 'Make It Funky (Pts 1 and 2)'. Polydor, 1971.
Brown, James. 'My Part/Make It Funky (Parts 3 and 4)'. Polydor, 1971.
Brown, James. *Revolution of the Mind – Live at the Apollo Vol. 3*. Polydor, 1971.
Brown, James. 'Get on the Good Foot'. Polydor, 1972.
Brown, James. 'Public Enemy #1, Pt.1' on *Star Time*. Polygram, 1972.
Brown, James. *Black Caesar*. Universal, 1973.
Brown, James. *Slaughter's Big Rip Off*. Universal, 1973.
Brown, James. 'Think'. Polydor, 1973.
Brown, James. 'Funky President' on *Reality*. Polydor, 1975.
Brown, James. 'Funky Drummer' on *In the Jungle Groove*. Polydor/Universal, 1986.
Brown, James. *I'm Real*. Scotti Bros, 1988.
Brown. James. *Live at the Apollo* (CD re-issue of 1963 album). Polygram, 1989.

Brown, James. *Roots of a Revolution*. Polygram, 1989.
Brown, James. 'Get It Together' on *Star Time*. Polygram, 1991.
Brown, James. *Hot Pants* (1991 re-issue). New York: Universal, 1991.
Brown, James 'Let Yourself Go' on *Star Time*. New York: Polygram, 1991.
Brown, James. *Star Time*. Polygram, 1991.
Brown, James. *Say It Live and Loud – Live in Dallas 08.26.68*. Polygram, 1995.
Brown, James. *Foundations of Funk – a Brand New Bag 1964–1969*. Polygram, 1996.
Brown, James. *Live at the Apollo Vol. 2 (Deluxe Edition)*. Universal, 2001.
Brown, James. *Funky People's Greatest Breakbeats*. Universal, 2005.
Brown, James. *Greatest Breakbeats*. Universal, 2005.
Brown, James and the Famous Flames. 'Please, Please, Please'. King, 1956.
Brown, James and the Louie Bellson Orchestra. *Soul on Top (2004 Reissue)*. Verve, 1969.
Cooke, Sam, 'A Change is Gonna Come' on *The Man and His Music*. RCA, 1986.
Davis, Miles. *Bitches Brew*. Columbia, 1969.
Davis, Miles. *On the Corner*. Columbia, 1972.
DJ Shadow. *Endtroducing*. Mo' Wax, 1996.
Edan the Deejay. 'Sound of the Funky Drummer' (uncredited "mixtape"), 2004.
Ghostface Killah. *Bulletproof Wallets*. Epic, 2001.
Jin. 'Learn Chinese'. EMI, 2004.
Kool Moe Dee. 'How Ya Like Me Now'. Jive, 1987.
LA Style. 'James Brown Is Dead'. Bounce Records, 1991.
Malcolm X. *Words from the Frontlines: Excerpts from the Great Speeches of Malcolm X*. BMG, 1992.
Nas. 'Get Down', *God's Son*. Sony, 2002.
Pete Rock, and CL Smooth. 'Da Two' on *Soul Survivor*. Loud Records, 1998.
Public Enemy. *It Takes a Nation of Millions To Hold Us Back*. Island/Def Jam, 1988.
Quasimoto. 'The Unseen' on *The Unseen*. Stones Throw, 2000.
Reich, Steve. *Early Works: Come out/PianoPhase/Clapping Music/It's Gonna Rain*. New York: Elektra/Nonesuch, 1987.
Sir Frontalot. 'Good Old Clyde'. Available online at http://frontalot.com, 2005.
Slum Village. 'I Don't Know' on *Fantastic Vol. 2*. Goodvibe, 2000.
Stetsasonic. 'Talkin' All That Jazz'. Tommy Boy, 1988.
Stubblefield, Clyde. *DNA Beat Blocks Groove Construction Kit: Clyde Stubblefield*. EastWest, 1993.
Stubblefield, Clyde. *Clyde Stubblefield: The Original*. Minnetonka: Liquid 8 Records, 2003.
Wagon Christ. 'Natural Suction' on *Musipal*. Ninja Tune, 2001.
Wu-Tang Clan. 'Method Man' on *Enter the 36 Chambers*. Loud Records, 1993.

Index

action-image   108, 120–23, 137, 139–40
'A Change is Gonna Come' (Sam Cooke)   14, 55–56, 60
activism   56, 71–72
affect   21–28, 35, 40, 48–49, 51–52, 54, 61, 65, 67–69, 75, 93, 95, 100, 102–103, 108, 112–13, 117–18, 120, 123, 125, 127, 130–31, 137, 140, 142–43, 145, 149
Afrika Bambaataa   126–27
Afrobeat   18
Afrocentrism   16, 41, 80
'Ain't It Funky Now' (James Brown)   107, 125
aion   110–11, 125, 131
'any-space-whatever'   140, 142
Apollo Theatre   1, 11, 57–59, 105, 124
'apprehension of a minor temporality'   20, 29, 50, 81, 105, 149
asignifying   24
assemblage   3, 39, 73, 81–82, 96, 106, 123, 131, 138, 147
Augé, Marc   139–40
Augusta, Georgia   1–2, 13, 31, 105, 114
authenticity   15, 66, 70, 77–78
Avons, The   33

Baadasssss (film)   121
'Baby Please Don't Go' (The Orioles)   33
Ballard, Hank   32, 34, 114, 117
Ballard, Hank and the Midnighters   32, 51
Banbarra   136
Baptist Church   36, 43, 79
Baraka, Amiri   37, 74
Barnwell, South Carolina   31
Barthes, Roland   66
Basquiat, Jean-Michel   121
bastardization   122, 131, 143, 150
Batey, Angus   127, 129
B-Boying   129

Beastie Boys, The   6, 91
Beatles, The   65, 150
beatmatching   137
bebop   74, 77, 90
becoming-music   48
becomings   14, 22, 66, 68–69, 93, 108, 113, 125, 139, 146
'Begging, Begging' (James Brown)   51
'belief in the body'   22, 68, 73, 76, 119
Bergson, Henri   29, 146
Berry, Chuck   62
Better Living Through Circuitry (film)   17
Big Daddy (magazine)   4, 136
Billboard (magazine)   56, 120
Bitches Brew (Miles Davis)   91
Biz Markie   6
Black Atlantic, The (book)   53, 79–81, 84, 92, 120
Black Eyed Peas, The   8
Black Panthers   114, 120
'Blackenized' (Hank Ballard)   117
'Blackie' (Hard-Ons, The)   73
blaxploitation   121–22
'Blind Man Can See It' (James Brown)   7
blues music and influence   2, 12, 31–33, 36–37, 52–53, 55–56, 66, 73, 77–79, 103, 107, 114, 120, 134
Bogue, Ronald   115
Bolden, Buddy   77
Bomb Squad, the   5
Brackett, David   14, 112
Bradley, Lloyd   133
breakbeat   4, 7, 125, 129–32, 136–37, 144
breakdancing   111, 129–30, 132
breakdown   111, 122, 130, 141
Brewster, Bill   4, 111, 127, 133, 135–37
Bronx, New York City   132–33, 142
Broughton, Frank   111, 127, 133, 135–37
Brown, Geoff   12, 51

Brown, James
    artists copying   5, 7
    as autocratic bandleader   85, 99
    band precision   16, 105
    childhood   31, 70, 79
    choreography   61, 64, 117
    crossover into pop   13, 58–59, 62–63, 70, 97, 116
    eccentricity   41
    as 'Godfather of Soul'   3, 11, 13–14, 54, 73, 77–78, 85, 88, 120, 142
    as 'Idiot'   88–89, 94, 96–97, 99–100, 118
    imitation   67–68, 149
    improvisation   14, 48, 50, 104, 111–12
    influence of preaching   42–44, 49, 109, 111–12
    influence of the church   36–37, 43–44, 46, 49–50, 53, 55, 74, 81, 109–11
    instrumental solos, soloing   42, 115, 117, 130
    'most sampled'   3, 9
    music and orthodoxy   89, 91, 97
    'Music Box' (in prison)   32
    musical innovation   2, 88–89, 96, 98, 100, 111
    musical precision   16–17
    naïvety and creativity   82, 88–90, 93–94, 97, 99–100
    New Orleans influence   3, 52, 77
    'One, the'   2–3, 14, 19, 21, 29, 40–41, 51, 59, 62, 82, 94, 101–103
    in prison   31–32, 43
    promoting 'blackness'   14, 23, 67, 70, 72–73, 121
    and race   70–72, 106
    relationship with Africa   3, 10, 13–16, 20, 37, 42, 44–45, 49–51, 54, 56, 61, 63, 71–72, 75, 78–81, 92, 97, 100–102, 105–106, 108–11, 113–15, 120–21, 127, 132, 143
    relationship with Georgia   1, 13, 32–33, 36
    stagecraft   62
    stamina   108
    stillborn birth   31
    in Vietnam   113–15
    vocal technique   32, 44, 75, 111, 124
    vocalizations   42, 74, 83, 86–87, 107, 112, 143
Burroughs, William S.   138
Byrd, Bobby   5, 32–33, 51, 64, 148

Cage, John   109
Cale, John   16
Caribbean, The   132–33
Carmichael, Stokely   71
Chambers, Iain   135
chance (in composition)   43, 89, 124
chaos   46–48, 89, 92, 95, 97, 138, 147
chaosmos   46–47, 92–96, 98, 147
Charles, Ray   18, 37, 53–55, 58, 62, 97
chitlin' circuit   57, 63
'Chonnie-on-Chon' (James Brown)   51
chromos   49, 110, 125, 131, 139, 143, 145
Cinema
    books   24–25, 28, 69, 101, 121
    Deleuze and theory   24–25, 28–29, 46, 50, 60–61, 69, 94–95, 100–101, 121, 123, 139–41, 143, 147
Civil Rights Act   56, 64
Civil rights movement   3, 19, 25, 27, 30, 37, 52–57, 74–75, 82, 90, 101, 114, 118, 120–21
Clinton, George   111, 126–27
'Cold Sweat' (James Brown)   2, 9, 20, 78, 83–84, 87, 124, 130, 148
Colebrook, Claire   144
Coleman, Ornette   74
collectivity   51, 56–57, 72, 96
Collins, Bootsy   127
colonialism   72
'Come Out' (Steve Reich)   109
composition   14, 18–19, 21, 23–25, 28–30, 33–34, 36, 40–41, 43, 45, 47–48, 50–52, 69, 77, 82, 84–85, 88, 90–91, 95–96, 103, 109, 111, 117, 124–25, 128, 131, 134–35, 137–38, 141, 147
compositional trajectory   43, 45–46, 51, 61, 82, 118, 120, 130–31
Cooke, Sam   54–55, 58
corporeal   22, 103
Cosmos   47
Count Basie   86
crystalline   40, 59, 143–44, 146
cut, the   7, 33, 42–47, 49–50, 65, 70, 81, 112, 125, 130–32, 136–38, 142

Index

D'Acquisto, Steve 137
Daedelus 7
Daltrey, Roger 65
dance 2, 4–7, 16–19, 23, 25, 27–28, 40, 42, 46, 48, 59, 73, 89, 97, 102–103, 108, 111–12, 117, 125, 127–29, 131–32, 134–39, 142, 147
Danielsen, Anne 13–14
'Da Two' (Pete Rock and CL Smooth) 7
Davis, Miles 14, 91–92
Debussy, Claude 26, 110
deindustrialism 121
De La Soul 6
Deleuze, Gilles 13, 19–25, 27–28, 30, 38–40, 45–50, 60–61, 67–71, 73, 88–90, 92–101, 109–10, 113, 121–24, 137, 139–43, 145–50
deterritorialization 39–40
Detroit 57, 114
Diaspora (African) 15, 73, 80, 105, 111
difference 13–14, 38, 47, 51, 60, 66–70, 75, 82–83, 88–89, 91, 94, 97–98, 143–47
digital technology 3–5, 123, 144
disco 12, 16, 108, 111, 124–27, 132–37, 150
DJ Shadow 4
DJs/DJing 3–4, 11, 25, 40, 57, 89, 112, 122–23, 125–32, 135–37, 141, 143, 145, 147, 149
DNA Beat Blocks (Clyde Stubblefield) 9
Doggett, Bill 58
'dogmatic image of thought' 88, 92, 94, 97–98, 123, 148, 150
Dorsey, Thomas 36–37
drums, drumming 3–5, 15, 17, 23, 42, 52, 74, 83, 85, 89, 92, 97–98, 106–107, 130, 132
Dunayevskaya, Raya 71
durée, duration 19, 29, 40, 48, 107, 131, 135, 138
Dyer, Richard 67
Dyke and the Blazers 83

Eckstine, Billy 58
Edan the Deejay 9
electronic music 4–6, 15–19, 23, 25, 97, 111, 131, 136, 138, 141
Eliot, Marc 11, 62–63, 102, 114
Ellis, Alfred 'Pee Wee' 3, 83, 85–86, 98

Endtroducing (DJ Shadow) 4
Eric B. and Rakim 5
Ertegun, Ahmet 53
'Escape-Ism' (James Brown) 148
essentialism 13–15, 23, 68, 78, 80, 92
ethnomusicology 81
ethology 22
Eurocentrism 80
Ever Ready Gospel Singers, The 33
Evers, Medger 120

Famous Flames, The 34, 63–64
Fillyau, Clayton 3, 52, 107
Five Royales, the 32, 52
Flaxman, Gregory 123
Flur, Wolfgang 17
Foulsham, Dom 2
Foundations of Funk, The (James Brown) 77, 87
Franklin, Aretha 43, 55, 61, 75, 84
Freed, Alan 146
Full Force 5
funk 2–4, 12–16, 18–21, 24–25, 27, 29–31, 40, 46–48, 51–52, 59, 73, 76–79, 81–87, 90–92, 94, 96, 98, 102–103, 105–10, 117–18, 123–24, 126–27, 130–31, 133–34
Funkadelic 16, 126–27
'Funky Butt' (Buddy Bolden) 77
'Funky Drummer' (James Brown) 4–5, 7–9, 23, 129–30, 147–49
'Funky President' (James Brown) 7, 115, 149

Garbage 9
Gaunt, Kyra 128
Gaye, Marvin 65, 74, 116
George, Nelson 13, 30, 103, 114, 120, 139
'Get Down' (Nas) 7, 42, 44
'Get It Together' (James Brown) 104
'Get on the Good Foot' (James Brown) 129
ghetto 114, 141–42, 148
Ghostface Killah 159
Gibbons, Walter 135
Gilbert, Jeremy 16, 26–27, 48
Gilroy, Paul 80–81, 92
'Give It up or Turnit-a-Loose' (James Brown) 125, 129, 132–33

Goldman, Albert   117
'Good Old Clyde' (Sir Frontalot)   9
Goodwin, Andrew   16
gospel   3, 33–37, 40–41, 43–44, 46–56, 60, 66, 75, 81–82, 110–12, 134
Gospel Starlighters, The   33
Gourevitch, Philip   35
Grandmaster Flash   3, 78, 127, 142
Grasso, Francis   127, 132, 135, 137
Great Depression, The   31, 36–37
Green, Al   18
groove   2, 4–6, 8, 13, 17, 25, 30, 46–47, 75, 78, 81–82, 90–92, 104–108, 111, 116, 122, 124–31, 133–35, 138–39, 141–42
Guattari, Félix   19–24, 26–27, 30, 38–40, 46–48, 67, 69, 71, 88, 90, 92–93, 95–97, 100, 109, 147, 150
Guralnick, Peter   3, 12, 15, 62–63, 84
Gysin, Brion   138

habit   38, 49–50, 94, 140
Haralambos, Michael   12, 44, 53, 55–56
Harlem, New York City   1, 58, 109, 114, 121
Harris, Wynonie   32
Headlam, Dave   66
Hegel   45
Hendrix, Jimi   81, 92
heterogeneity   7, 68, 109, 139
hip-hop   3–7, 9, 16, 18, 26, 40, 77, 95, 111, 117, 125, 127–33, 137, 141–42, 147
Hirshey, Gerri   12, 36–37, 53–54, 56–57, 63, 70–72, 104, 120
Horne, Lena   72
Hoskyns, Barney   41
'Hot Pants' (James Brown)   134, 148
'How You Gonna Get Respect (When You Haven't Cut Your Process Yet)' (Hank Ballard)   117
Howlin' Wolf   37

'I Don't Know' (Slum Village)   34, 79
'I Got the Feelin'' (James Brown)   9, 133
'I Got You (I Feel Good)' (James Brown)   11, 55, 82, 102, 114, 127
'I'll Go Crazy' (James Brown)   52
'I'm Real' (James Brown with Full Force)   5–6
'I'm Tired but I'm Clean' (James Brown)   118

incorporeal   22
industrialism   7, 32, 105–106, 121
the intolerable   25, 30, 48, 100–101, 108, 123, 140
irrational cut   25, 43, 45–47, 50, 112, 122, 125, 128–31, 134, 137–39, 141, 144
Isley Brothers, The   44
'It's Gonna Rain' (Steve Reich)   109
It Takes a Nation of Millions to Hold Us Back (Public Enemy)   5–6, 147–48
'I've Got Money' (James Brown)   3, 52, 82

Jackson, Mahalia   36–37
Jackson, Michael   1, 63
Jagger, Mick   64
James Brown in the Jungle Groove (James Brown)   4, 8
'James Brown is Dead' (LA Style)   1, 6
James Brown's Greatest Breakbeats (James Brown)   4
jazz   3, 5, 26, 37, 50–51, 53–54, 74, 77–78, 85–86, 90, 92, 97, 104–105, 111, 130
JBs, The   115, 127–28, 142
Jin (hip-hop artist)   7
Johnson, Lyndon   64, 113
Jones, LeRoi *see also* Amiri Baraka   36–37, 74

Kafka, Franz   38–40
Kellum, Alphonso 'Country'   103
Kendricks, Eddie   111
Keyes, Cheryl   77
King, Martin Luther   101, 113, 120, 141
King Records   34
King Tubby   133
Kingston, Jamaica   133
Kofsky, Frank   77
Kool Herc   126–27, 129, 131–32
K-OS   7
Kraftwerk   17, 141
KRS-One   127
Ku Klux Klan   124
Kumar, Shiv   29

Lascaibar, 'Legs'   129
LA Style (group)   1, 149
Law, John   72, 109–10
'Learn Chinese' (Jin)   7

Index

Lechte, John   100
Led Zeppelin   17
Leeds, Alan   8, 13, 20, 44, 58
Leibniz   122
'Let a Man Come in and Do the Popcorn' (James Brown)   117
'Let Yourself Go' (James Brown)   107
Levine, Sherrie   144
linearity (in music)   13, 25, 29–30, 41, 47, 50, 60–61, 75, 80, 82, 111, 122, 125, 130–31, 134, 137–38, 143
Live at the Apollo (James Brown)   1, 11, 57–59, 105, 124
'Living in America' (James Brown)   1
Living in America: The Soul Saga of James Brown (book)   7, 11
Lyotard, Jean-François   101

Maben, Adrian   31, 104
machinic   17–18, 28, 106, 112
Macon, Georgia   33
major, majoritarian   5–6, 8, 12, 16, 18, 22, 36, 38–40, 49–50, 67, 71–73, 75, 78, 93, 101–102, 104, 114,   116, 133, 141, 149–50
'Make It Funky' (James Brown)   78, 134, 139
Malcolm X   56, 115, 120
Mark Anthony Neal   30, 61, 102, 120
Marsalis, Wynton   92
Marxism   71
Massumi, Brian   24, 140, 147
Maycock, James   113
melisma   44
melody   35, 47, 83, 103–105, 131
Messing with the Blues (James Brown)   33
Meters, The   126
'Method Man' (Wu-Tang Clan)   131
micropolitics   61, 75
Middleton, Richard   45
minimalism   106–10
minor   18, 20, 22, 25, 29, 38–40, 44, 46–51, 54, 65, 69–72, 74–75, 81–83, 90, 93–94, 96–97, 100, 102, 105, 108, 110, 115, 119, 139, 143, 145, 147–50
minority   20, 25, 38–40, 44, 46, 71, 74–75, 94, 100, 102, 115, 149
modernism   61, 101
Mods   65

modulation   28, 35
Modulations (book)   130
Mojo (magazine)   133
molar   140
molecular   19
Moog synthesizer   15
Morgan, Robert P.   109
Morrison, Van   86
Morton, Jelly Roll   77
Motown   64, 97, 133
Moulton, Tom   135–36
movement-image   24–25, 28, 46, 50, 60, 93, 105, 108, 110, 122, 125, 131, 137, 139
Muhammad Ali   114
musicology   13, 14, 112
Musik (magazine)   147
Musipal (Wagon Christ)   7

Nas   7
Nathan, Syd   34, 44, 57, 59
'Natural Suction' (Wagon Christ)   7
Neal, Mark Anthony   30, 56, 61, 102, 120–22
Nietzsche, Friedrich   122, 146, 148
'Night of the Living Baseheads' (Public Enemy)   148
'Night Train' (James Brown)   52, 63, 89
Nixon, Richard   114
Nolen, Jimmy   103, 106

Ogg, Alex   127, 132
'Oh Baby Don't You Weep' (James Brown)   44, 82
On the Corner (Miles Davis)   91
ontology   11, 16, 19–20, 22, 25, 28, 30
Orioles, The   33
'Out of Sight' (James Brown)   3, 59, 63, 82–83

Palmer, Robert   3, 78, 104
'Papa's Got a Brand New Bag' (James Brown)   2–3, 17, 19–20, 60, 75, 82–83, 102
Parker, Maceo   77, 85, 104, 127–28
Parker, Melvin   121
Parliament   13, 16, 126–27
Parnet, Claire   19
'Pass the Peas' (The JBs)   8

Patton, Paul   72, 144–45
'The Payback' (James Brown)   91
Payne, Jim   107–108
Pearson, Iain   16
Peebles, Ann   121
Pentecostal church   109
periodicities   49
Perry, Lee 'Scratch'   133
Pete Rock and CL Smooth   7
Pickett, Wilson   18, 83
Plato, Platonism   144–45, 147
Platters, The   58
'Please, Please, Please' (James Brown and the Famous Flames)   33–35, 41, 44, 46, 51, 57, 63, 82
Polygram Records   4, 6, 87
polyphony   15
polyrhythms   104, 134
'The Popcorn' (James Brown)   117
Poschardt, Ulf   77, 134
postcolonial   143
postmodernism   7, 13, 28, 101, 144
post-soul   25, 30, 120–28, 131, 138–39, 141–43, 148–49
poststructuralism   24, 26, 28
powers of the false   7, 15, 40, 93, 122, 143–47, 149
Presley, Elvis   63
Priestley, Philip   120
Prince   111
'Prisoner of Love' (James Brown)   58–59, 63
Public Enemy   4, 6, 44, 77, 127, 147–48
'Public Enemy #1' (James Brown)   44
Puritanism   73, 101

Quasimoto   7

race riots   114, 116, 141
Rainey, Ma   36
Rajchman, Jonathan   69, 88, 94, 110, 118
rap   9, 44, 111, 134
Reagan, Ronald   121, 139
'Reaganomics'   121
'Rebel Without a Pause' (Public Enemy)   147
Redding, Otis   55, 75
Reed, Waymond   85–86

refrain   50, 82, 149
reggae   132–33
Reich, Steve   109
Reid, Vernon   121
reification   15
remix, remixing   129, 133–36, 143, 147
repetition   13, 30, 40–47, 49–50, 52, 67–68, 81–82, 88, 100, 103, 105, 109–10, 112, 131–32, 134, 144, 146–47, 149
representation   21–23, 26, 28, 35, 67–71, 73, 113, 122, 143–45, 147–50
reterritorialization   40, 143
Reynolds, Simon   27, 112–13
Rhizomatics   48
Rhodes, Don   13, 15
rhythm   2–3, 14, 16–18, 20, 29, 32, 37, 40, 43, 45, 47, 50, 52, 74, 78–79, 83, 90, 92, 102–104, 106–107, 114, 120, 125, 130, 134, 142
Richardson, Dorothy   29
Riley, Terry   109
Roach, Max   86
Robinson, Smokey   62, 64, 74
rock'n'roll   7, 36, 72–73, 121, 129
Rodowick, D. N.   29, 46, 61, 122, 125–26, 138, 143, 146
Rolling Stone (magazine)   9–10
Rolling Stones, The   62–65
Roots, The   5, 11, 35, 53
Rose, Cynthia   7, 11, 13, 41, 81, 97–98, 111, 134
Rose, Tricia   16, 142
Rosselini, Roberto   100

samples, sampling   3–9, 11–12, 16, 23–24, 40, 89, 112, 122–23, 125, 128, 131, 136, 141, 143–50
Satie, Erik   110
'Say it Loud—I'm Black and I'm Proud' (James Brown)   56, 70–71, 103, 114, 116–18
Schaeffer, Pierre   18
Schoenberg, Arnold   37
scratch, scratching   103, 105, 133, 136
seer   93–94
sensation (in art)   21–22, 95
sensorimotor   61, 122
serial, seriality   134, 143, 145

Index

series   11–13, 28, 31, 42, 50, 59–60, 64, 66, 89, 96, 105, 124, 137, 141, 143, 148
sex, sexuality   71–73, 77
Sex Machine (James Brown)   73, 103, 129, 132, 134
Sharp, Chris   130
Sharpton, Al   72
Sherrell, 'Sweet' Charles   116
Shindig   127
Shocklee, Hank   5, 95
'Shout and Shimmy' (James Brown)   44
Showtime (James Brown)   59
Sidran, Ben   54–55, 73–74, 101–102
signs and signification   23, 26–27, 68, 129, 138
Simins, Russel   9, 85
simulacra, simulacrum   145–50
Sinatra, Frank   59, 96
singles (45s)   5, 14, 20, 44, 52, 82–83, 129, 133–35
Sir Frontalot   9
slavery   95
Smith, Huey 'Piano' and the Clowns   3
SNCC   71
Snead, James   41–42, 44–45
soul   2–3, 5–7, 11–15, 18, 25, 30–31, 33, 35, 37, 44, 51–57, 60–65, 73–75, 77–78, 83–85, 88, 90, 92, 100–102, 104, 118, 120–28, 131, 134, 136, 138–39, 141–44, 148–49
Soul Brother No. 1   12, 31, 54
'Soul Pride' (James Brown)   117
Soul Survivor (Pete Rock)   7
Sound of the Funky Drummer (Edan the DJ)   8–9
soundscape   19, 109, 148
South, the (Southern United States)   31, 34, 105, 142
Spinoza   24, 68
spiritual automaton   28, 93
Starks, John 'Jabo'   85, 103, 107, 128
Star Time (James Brown)   8, 107
Stax Records   120
Steinski   136
Stetsasonic   5, 8
Stockhausen, Karlheinz   18, 91
Stone, Sly   9–10, 91–92, 126
stratification   38, 70, 73

stream of consciousness   29
structuralism   28
Stubblefield, Clyde   8–9, 103, 106–107, 130, 132
Sullivan, Ed   6, 70, 74, 127
'Superbad' (James Brown)   14, 112
Supremes, The   62
Surfin' (The Beach Boys)   58
Sweetback Sweetback's Baadasssss Song (film)   121
syncreticism   81
synthesis   15, 21, 50, 141

Tagg, Philip   14
Tampa Red   31, 36
Taylorism   106
techno   1, 6, 105, 125, 132
teens, teenagers   32, 58, 62–63, 72, 83
teleological   25, 30, 41, 46, 49–51, 60–61, 75, 90, 101, 109–10, 118–19, 121–23
telos   25, 45, 52, 60, 75, 110, 124, 126
tempo   42, 56
temporal   24–25, 28, 41, 48–50, 60, 109, 111, 122–23, 135, 138, 144–45
temporality   13, 20, 25, 29, 38, 47, 49–50, 75, 81, 94, 102, 105, 125, 138, 141, 149
Temptations, The   111
Terminator X   148
territorialization   24, 40, 48
Tex, Joe   34
Tharpe, Sister Rosetta   36
'There Was a Time' (James Brown)   105, 124
'They Don't Want Music' (Black Eyed Peas)   8
'Think (About It)'   5, 7, 149
Thompson, Ahmir 'Questlove'   5
Thousand Plateaus, A (book)   24, 38
timbre   16–17, 42
time   1–2, 5–6, 8–9, 11–13, 17, 19–21, 25, 28–32, 36–38, 41, 43–44, 46–51, 53, 56, 58, 60–62, 65–66, 71, 73–75, 79, 81, 83–85, 90, 92, 100–11, 116, 118, 121–28, 131, 133, 136–41, 143–47, 149
time-image   24–25, 28, 46, 50, 100, 108–10, 121, 123, 125–26, 131, 137, 139–41, 143–44, 146–47
Toccoa, Georgia   32–33

Toop, David 131
transcendence 48, 88, 139
transcendental 29, 46, 48, 52, 55, 96, 118
transgression 32, 48
transversal, transversality 143, 147
Trenchtown, (Kingston, Jamaica) 141
Trick Daddy 7
'Try Me' (James Brown) 51–52
Tucker, Bruce 11, 32–33, 58–59, 79
turntable 128, 131
'Tutti Frutti' (Little Richard) 71–72

Uncut (magazine) 41
unorthodox, unorthodoxy 11, 51, 87–89
Unseen, The (Quasimoto) 7

vamping (music) 47, 105, 124, 134
Velvet Underground 16
Vincent, Ricky 12, 15–16, 18, 71, 78–79, 114–17
vinyl records 129
virtual, the 25, 48–49, 62, 75, 138, 140, 144, 147
virtuosity 51, 87, 90–91, 97, 104
voice 5, 15, 55, 58, 61, 66, 83, 104, 109, 112

Waddy, Frank 'Kash' 127
Wagon Christ 7
warehouse parties 140–41
Warhol, Andy 7
Watergate scandal 115
Watts riots 114
Wax Poetics (magazine) 4, 116
WDIA (radio station) 57
Weinger, Harry 4, 8, 12, 20, 51, 84, 107, 113
Werner, Craig 14, 65, 91–92, 135
Wesley, Fred 9, 12, 43, 84–86, 98, 124, 127
Wexler, Jerry 84, 120
White, Cliff 8, 12, 33, 51, 83, 113, 150
Whitfield, Norman 111
Who, The 4, 65, 95
WIBB (radio station) 33
'will to power' 122
Wolk, Douglas 11, 34
Wonder, Stevie 116
Woolf, Virginia 29
Wu-Tang Clan 131
Wyman, Bill 63

Young, LaMonte 109

www.ingramcontent.com/pod-product-compliance
Lightning Source LLC
Chambersburg PA
CBHW051128160426
43195CB00014B/2387